THREE SEASONS
IN THE WIND

950 Kilometres by Canoe
Down Northern Canada's Thelon River

by
Kathleen Pitt and Michael Pitt

Second Edition

Hornby House

Canadian Cataloguing in Publication Data

Pitt, Kathleen, 1952-
    Three seasons in the wind

    Includes bibliographical references.
    ISBN 0-9686581-0-5

    1. Pitt, Kathleen, 1952- --Journeys. 2. Pitt,Michael D. --Journeys. 3.
Thelon River (N.W.T. and Nunavut)--Description and travel. 4. Canoes and
canoeing--Thelon River (N.W.T. and Nunavut) I. Pitt, Michael D. II. Title.
GV776.15.N57P57 2000   797.1'22'097194 C00-910081-4

Distributed by **Gordon Soules Book
Publishers Ltd**. ● 1359 Ambleside Lane,
West Vancouver, BC, Canada V7T 2Y9
● PMB 620, 1916 Pike Place #12,
Seattle, WA 98101-1097 US
E-mail: books@gordonsoules.com
Web site: http://www.gordonsoules.com
(604) 922 6588 Fax: (604) 688 5442

HORNBY HOUSE PUBLICATIONS
1723 Torquay Avenue, North Vancouver, BC V7J 1R6, Canada

Book design, illustrations and maps by Nola Johnston
Cover photos by Michael Pitt
All other photos by Kathleen Pitt or Michael Pitt

Printed in Canada

DEDICATION

We wish to dedicate this book to our parents: to my father, William Pitt, for introducing me to the joy of wilderness life and travel; *and to my father and mother, Joe and Terry Hynes, for supporting and encouraging me in this adventure, despite their misgivings and concerns for my safety.*

DISCLAIMER

Neither the authors, Kathleen Pitt and Michael Pitt, nor the publisher, shall have any liability or responsibility to any person with respect to loss or damage caused or alleged to be caused directly or indirectly by information contained in this book. It is the sole responsibility of the paddler to determine whether or not he/she is qualified to safely navigate any fast water situations, to safely live in wilderness conditions, and to accurately assess present conditions in relation to published material.

We can not be responsible for the safety of groups travelling down the Thelon River or any other river. All paddlers must realize that paddling wilderness rivers is an inherently risky activity. Do not participate in this activity without first gaining appropriate wilderness and paddling skills. You must have an understanding of the risks involved and personally assume responsibility for all the risks. Rivers may change significantly from season to season, and from year to year. The decision of the group, and of individuals, to run any rapid should be based on a visual inspection of the rapid. Before choosing to run any rapid, all paddlers must individually assess the skill level of all group members versus the hazards that present themselves. Such hazards and assessments include water volume and air temperature, skills, fatigue, amount of freeboard, degree of isolation, risk to personal equipment, and feasibility or likelihood of rescue. There is no substitute for skill, preparedness, and good judgement.

CONTENTS

PREFACE

As we write this introduction, Kathleen and I speculate what has prompted you, the potential reader, to pick up our book, and leaf through its pages. Are you seeking solace in the aisles of the nation's paddling stores, trying to escape vicariously from the grey, frozen months of winter? Are you planning and dreaming of your own wilderness canoe trip down one of Canada's unlimited, pristine waterways? Are you fascinated by the history, lore and lure of Canada's tundra landscape? Are you wondering what kinds of physical and canoeing skills are required to travel freely and alone, for nearly six weeks, surrounded only by wind, water, and wildlife?

If you answered yes to any of these questions, then we invite you to pour a cup of tea or glass of brandy, curl up in your favorite chair, and share our experiences on one of Canada's most magnificent wilderness rivers. The Thelon River, part of the Canadian Heritage Rivers System, flows 950 km across Northern Canada's Barren Grounds, between Great Slave Lake and Baker Lake, at the head of Chesterfield Inlet on Hudson Bay.

In the summer of 1993, Kathleen and I lived like nomads, while we paddled with whim and purpose down the Thelon River. Our chartered Cessna 185 landed on Lynx Lake, near the river's outlet, on June 28. Ice still choked most of the lake's surface. Red-pink mats of alpine azaleas revealed the buds of a new Arctic spring. From the moment we paddled through the outlet, wind became our constant companion and adversary throughout our journey. Thirty-seven days later, on a cobble beach below Aleksektok Rapids, we lingered silently over our last breakfast on the river. We harvested blueberries, loaded the canoe, and paddled the final 80 km to Baker Lake beneath rainy, somber, fall-like skies.

Three Seasons in the Wind presents our thoughts and feelings during those brief, memorable weeks on the Barren Grounds. We chose to paddle alone, to truly experience the isolation of Canada's uninhabited, seemingly endless, tundra landscape.

Our story is based on personal diaries, in which we confided privately, while resting in the evening tent, pitched on riverside beach, terrace boulder field, or esker ridge. We kept our diaries secret from each other until returning to Vancouver. Reading to each other at home, our diaries confirmed that Kathleen and I recorded our daily experiences differently, because of our distinct personal history and perspectives. By merging both diaries, *Three Seasons in the Wind* presents a complementary account of our summer on the Thelon River. I present my view from the stern in Roman type, while Kathleen's observations from the bow are displayed in *italics*.

Although our summer canoeing holiday seems rather humble to Michael and me, our families and many of our friends consider the trip adventurous enough to have suggested that we write this book. We appreciate their support and encouragement. We particularly hope that our accounts convince them, and you, that canoeing across the Barren Grounds represents a modern-day, mini-adventure attainable by virtually everyone.

Michael and I are neither athletic nor superbly conditioned. At the time of our trip in 1993, we were both in our forties, and well past our collective physical prime. We first began canoeing in 1987, primarily because backpacking was becoming increasingly more difficult. I remember one particularly arduous backpacking trip into the southern Yukon's Tombstone Range in the summer of 1986. After struggling through 2 km of dense willows and bog birch, we reached the last ridge before our intended evening camp. Through eyes of fatigue, we gazed down a broad valley, bisected by a wide river flowing easily toward the northern Yukon horizon.

Suddenly the light of logic and reason shone upon us! Certainly, floating through the wilderness would be infinitely easier than labouring uphill beneath heavy loads that granted only 7-10 days escape from urban noise and concrete.

Michael and I regularly give slide shows on wilderness canoeing to clubs and groups throughout Vancouver. At a presentation last spring, we were particularly gratified when an audience member confided that one of our previous slide shows had motivated her to canoe the Bowron Lakes. She once again sat in our audience, hoping that her friends would be similarly inspired to join her in paddling the Nahanni River.

Kathleen and I entertain similar ambitions for this book. We invite you to paddle the Thelon River with us, and to share our evening campsites. Only occasionally do we interject our opinions and philosophy of wilderness canoeing, which we hope are relevant to your personal canoeing aspirations. Most of all, though, we hope to inspire readers to cast your visions northward, to seek your own pleasures and rewards in Canada's vast Arctic landscapes.

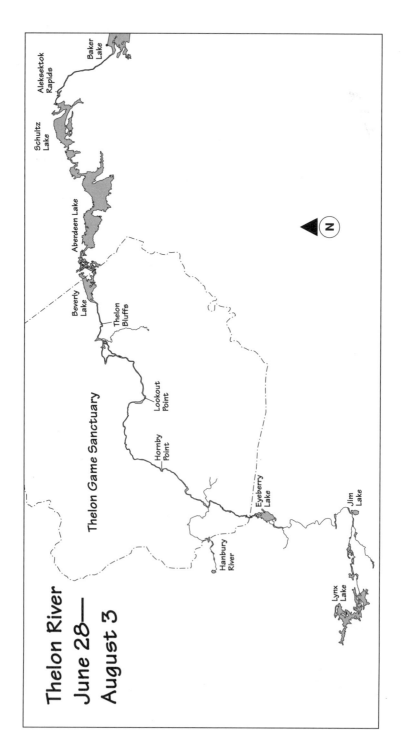

Thelon River
June 28—
August 3

Thelon Game Sanctuary

N

Baker Lake
Aleksektok Rapids
Schultz Lake
Aberdeen Lake
Beverly Lake
Thelon Bluffs
Lookout Point
Hornby Point
Eyeberry Lake
Jim Lake
Hanbury River
Lynx Lake

IN THE BEGINNING

January 1993

Kathleen and I had never heard of the Thelon River until 1991. Yet, for the past 18 months, I have been absorbed by its lure. The river consumes all my free thoughts. Several logical and emotional reasons explain my fascination with this largest river in the Northwest Territories flowing into Hudson Bay. Since 1986, after my first trip north of 60 degrees latitude, I have been intrigued with Canada's northern landscape, particularly the Barren Grounds. Historically, this limitless region north of tree line created awe and fear in the few Europeans who penetrated its frontiers. Any realm with such power must contain magical qualities.

The Thelon River also provides one of the longest wilderness canoe trips available in Canada, traversing 950 km between the sub-Arctic forest east of Great Slave Lake to Baker Lake, at the head of Chesterfield Inlet. Along the way, the canoeist encounters several portages and three large tundra lakes. Native peoples hunted and fished along the water's edge, leaving behind stone Inukshuks as reminders of their vibrant existence. An isolated stand of spruce trees shelters the graves of John Hornby, Edgar Christian and Harold Adlard, who struggled poignantly before they starved to death during an unforgiving Barren Grounds winter of 1926-27. Meandering between 62 and 64 degrees north, the Thelon blesses the summer canoeist with nearly constant daylight. The river's middle section flows through the Thelon Game Sanctuary, home to approximately 2000 muskoxen, which still graze freely on the Barren Grounds, as they have since the great glaciers melted 6,000-10,000 years ago. How could there be a better trip in Canada? How could one be a Canadian and a canoeist, and not want to paddle the Thelon?

The book *Nastawgan*, meaning "the ways" or "the routes," provides an intriguing series of essays describing the wilderness canoe trip in terms of the heroic quest. The essays begin with an introduction by P.E. Trudeau, well known, not only for his political success, but also for his lifelong devotion to canoeing:

> "What sets a canoeing expedition apart is that
> it purifies you more rapidly and inescapably
> than any other. Travel a thousand miles by
> train and you are a brute; pedal five hundred
> on a bicycle and you remain a bourgeois; pad-
> dle a hundred in a canoe and you are already a
> child of nature."

Modern transportation subjugates nature to technology. Mechanized transportation penetrates and subdues the environment. Canoeing, in marked contrast, sets the quester upon the water environment, which immediately envelops and transports the adventurer. Paddling merely acts to deflect or modify the direction and speed of the canoe, which floats, as one, with the pulsing, living water.

Many of our friends, and most of our family, advise that we take a radio for emergencies. Although we will pack an

Emergency Position Indicating Radio Beacon (EPIRB) as insurance against life-threatening circumstances, we reject the recommendation to take a radio. The Thelon River represents our personal quest, and all quests must contain four ingredients: separation; trial; victories of initiation; and, triumphant return to society.

A radio diminishes our quest, which demands that Kathleen and I separate from civilization. If we can order a pizza, hail a cab, or call time out, then we haven't really separated. We need to stand alone on the endless tundra. We want to view our part of a remote, isolated world. We seek the satisfaction and strength that are derived from living and surviving in that isolation.

Kathleen and I have chosen to paddle alone down the Thelon River primarily to experience and to appreciate the loneliness and the vastness of the Barren Grounds. We want the Barrens to surround us—to envelop us—to embrace us. We desire to understand the words of Saltatha, a Yellowknife Dene, responding to a 19th Century missionary:

> "My father, you have spoken well; you have told me that Heaven is very beautiful; tell me now one more thing. Is Heaven more beautiful than the country of the muskox in summer, when sometimes the mist blows over the lakes, and sometimes the water is blue, and the loons cry very often?"

This magical solitude of the Barren Grounds is likely best absorbed in the quiet, private reflection of our own company.

The Inuit of the open tundra named the Thelon "Ark-i-Linik," or "wooded river." This historical name held promise that we would be able to find firewood for cooking as we pass through the Barren Grounds. We had also read that oases of spruce forest line the river's banks from Lynx Lake to Beverly Lake. Nonetheless, we felt very uncomfortable embarking on a Barren Grounds trip for the first time, not knowing if there would be sufficient wood for meals and washing. We had decided to take two one-burner backpacking stoves, with the extra stove providing an additional burner, and emergency back-up if the first stove malfunctioned. The "burning" question plagued us for weeks. How much fuel should we take? Too much would mean needless weight and bulk on the portages, but too little fuel put us at risk of eating cold, unpalatable food.

We decided to experiment on a snowy day in February. Air temperature equaled only 4° C, which I hoped would simulate the coldest weather that we might encounter on the Thelon River. For our trial, we prepared a sample day of meals, including four boiled pots of water for tea and soup, one breakfast bannock, and one dinner. To create even more realistic conditions, I filled a small pot with water, wedged the pot into a snow bank beneath our back yard maple tree, and waited for 30 minutes.

The first pot of water boiled in 6 minutes, at near full power. Approximately 1 additional minute was lost to windscreen fiddling and pumping a stubborn flame into life. To the second pot of water, I added a little snow for special effect. A more prolonged boiling, to kill potential bacteria that might infest the Thelon River, required seven minutes.

We then decided it might be more fuel-efficient to boil large pots of water. I now poured twice the amount of water into our biggest pot. Two full pots boiled in a total of 17 minutes, and provided enough water for tea, oatmeal, and washing. Bannock averaged 23 minutes to cook to a golden brown on both sides. The spaghetti dinner consumed 27 minutes of fuel.

These 67 minutes did not deplete all the fuel in the stove, meaning that we could supply more than one day's needs with a single filling. Our Coleman Peak 1 holds 335.3 ml, and is rated to burn one hour and 15 minutes at full power. If each day required a full stove, we would need 14 litres of white gas for the 42-day trip. Because we needed less than one stove per day, we decided to take two 4-litre cans of white gas, plus three 1-litre fuel bottles and two filled stoves for a total of 11.7 liters. We also assumed that some wood would likely be available for the first three weeks, until we reached the true tundra at Beverly Lake.

June 1993

Food has literally consumed my thoughts for these last six months before our trip begins. The caloric and nutritional values of food obviously assume paramount importance for our expedition. Food also brings enjoyment and comfort, which are vital for our emotional well being. This is especially so on the extended wilderness trip ahead of us, where so much is unfamiliar.

At first I thought only of the big picture. What general attributes would our food need in the context of this trip? We expect a small supply of wood on the Barrens; our menus, therefore, should require minimal cooking at mealtime. Space in the canoe is limited; the food must be compact and as light as possible. We intend to take 42 days of meals—variety in size and shape as well as in the ingredients themselves is needed to maintain interest and enjoyment.

Next I began to compile a plan for the dinners. I read and re-read menus and tips recommended in backpacking cookbooks. Over several months, I prepared sample meals, dried them, rehydrated them, and heated them to test their suitability. I noted the amount of each ingredient required in dried form.

I generally achieved my best results by preparing and drying each ingredient individually. I then combined and packaged these ingredients together to form complete meals. To develop the best spicing for our riverside dishes, I experimented with packaged sauce mixes. My shopping trips to the grocery store lengthened as I read the ingredients and instructions of gravy mixes and spaghetti sauces. Eventually I was rewarded by finding a spaghetti sauce that could be prepared without adding tomato sauce. One less ingredient to dry, package and portage!

I learned that almost any meal normally prepared at home could be adapted for our trip, and that thin uniform pieces of food dry and rehydrate best. Ground beef provides an excellent base for many meals, including chili, meat sauce and shepherd's pie, and is very easy to dry in the oven.

With experimentation now complete, I chose 7 recipes, each of which will be repeated several times throughout the trip: chili, shepherd's pie, Moroccan chicken stew, Szechuan stir-fry, spaghetti, beef stew and baked beans. To complete these menus I added cornbread to the chili, dumplings to the beef stew, rice to the stir-fry, and couscous to the Moroccan chicken stew. The variety of textures in these foods, such as shredded beef and carrots in Szechuan stir-fry and the large slices of carrots, potatoes, parsnips and beef in the beef stew, will maintain interest and enjoyment throughout the trip. All these foods will be completely cooked before drying, which fulfills the requirement for fuel efficiency.

I want our lunches on the river to be hot, easy to prepare, and quick to eat. Cup-of-soup and Japanese-style noodles provided perfect solutions. Both can be prepared with water boiled at breakfast, and then kept hot until noon in our thermos. Crackers with peanut butter and cheese and bags of jerky and dried fruits will complete our lunch menus.

Breakfast menus proved easier than lunch or dinner. Oatmeal is quick, and hot. Bannock with butter and jam will give us the feeling of eating fresh bread. I included granola for those meals that we might want to prepare and eat quickly, such as on rainy mornings, or at the end of particularly difficult days.

Dried foods all lack fat. For lunch, especially on cold days, I've included fatty sausages for added calories. Chickpeas in the chili, and dried figs and prunes add fiber to our diet. To ensure our nutritional health, we will also take a daily multivitamin to complement the vitamins contained in our dried fruits and vegetables.

I also added extra treats to the menus. Dried bananas and pineapple rings, with or without a sugar syrup dip, produced candy-like results. I experimented with different kinds of crackers to complement peanut butter or cheese for lunch. Graham wafers kept well, without crumbling. From the deli, I acquired small cocktail breads to add variety to lunches.

I purchased a small food dryer to use in combination with my kitchen oven. The oven worked best for ground meats, tomato leathers, and vegetables cut in small pieces. Jerky and large slices of vegetables dehydrated best in the food dryer.

I prepared a master list of all ingredients that we would need for all our meals. During each visit to the store, I purchased some beef for jerky, or ground chicken or beef for drying. I also bought vegetables and fruits to place into the food dehydrator. Slowly, our freezer filled with neatly packaged bundles of dried food.

Once the provisions were purchased and prepared, I faced the task of packaging. While Michael travelled to Kenya on business for three weeks last month, I spent most of my time packaging food. I gathered together my recipe lists, measuring cups and spoons, ingredients, bags for packaging, and paper on which to write instructions. Soon, one of the distinct meals was ready, followed by a second, then a third. I made 44 recipes of bannock, and packaged each in a plastic bag closed with a twist tie. Supplementary foods such as milk powder, sugar and flour were packaged separately.

I especially enjoyed making our gorp snacks. At a bulk food store, I bought a couple of pounds each of nuts, raisins, yogurt-covered raisins, M&Ms, pretzels, sesame sticks, and licorice allsorts. At home, I mixed these ingredients in a large tub before dividing them into 84 little, separate, plastic bags.

A mountain of food now lay in the centre of our living room floor. To this heap, I finally added the perishables—cheese, margarine and sausages. Would this all fit into the packs? Have I forgotten something important? In less than a week, we will leave Vancouver for Fort Smith and the Thelon River!

Saturday, June 19

Only a few days, now, before we leave. Yesterday, the last Friday for eight weeks at my office at the University of British Columbia kept me very busy. I dispatched seemingly endless numbers of memos and reports that could, and should, have been finished days, even weeks ago. I must still return to the office tomorrow to write two letters of recommendation, complete a curriculum report, and prepare a list of instructions to ensure the orderly arrival of four Kenyans beginning their graduate studies at UBC in early August. I'm feeling a bit tired, and look forward to a relaxing week during our drive to Fort Smith.

Although I'm tired mostly mentally, I'm also physically weary after a 12-hour day of lawn-mowing, weeding, watering, and pruning shrubs and trees. Vacations are always hectic, particularly those that retreat to the wilderness. Last evening we filled the canoe packs, which fortunately fit easily below the gunwales, and our spray deck snapped tightly in place. We're ready to go, after 18 months of planning!

This quiet moment before departure is always difficult emotionally, as I take great pleasure and satisfaction in my garden, which is now manicured perfectly, with no major tasks remaining. I think how nice it would be to stay home, to sit comfortably surrounded by my flowers, and enjoy the long summer progression into fall harvests of tomatoes, sweetpeas, and aromatic herbs. Our Thelon trip will take us away from all these domestic pleasures, and thrust us into rapids, hordes of biting insects and potentially life-threatening winds on Aberdeen Lake. Schultz Lake outlet may still be blocked by ice. Aleksektok Rapids may be filled with crashing blocks of careening ice, as described in Chris Norment's book *In the North of our Lives*.

I empathize with Bilbo Baggins. Kathleen and I are really a Hobbit couple, happiest at home with our cakes and teas. Like Bilbo and his friends, though, we are invariably drawn, against our wishes, into journeys and adventures through unknown lands.

Monday, June 21

We have just finished our "last" supper—barbecued steaks in the back yard. We're watching our last Atlanta Braves baseball game on TBS until mid-August. Tomorrow morning, we'll be on our way to begin the biggest adventure of our lives together. All our food is ready and packed. All our gear fits in the canoe, even with the spray cover snapped in place. Even so, I don't feel completely ready, and I have very mixed emotions.

Mom and Dad have been very good about this trip. Despite their worries and concern about us, they have shown real interest and enthusiasm. We gave Dad maps and the itinerary of our Thelon River journey, and he plans to plot our daily route. Today, they stopped by with lunch from MacDonald's, plus treats of candy, gum, nuts and cheese for us to eat on the way to Fort Smith. Displaying his Victoria naval tradition, Dad requested an official inspection of gear. I hope they felt reassured by seeing the first aid kit and all the provisions that we have prepared for the journey.

As they said good-bye for the summer, I silently wished I too were staying home to follow our itinerary on the maps. I would enjoy hearing all about the river quest, once it had been safely concluded. At the present moment the security of home exerts a stronger pull for me than the adventure we have been planning for 18 months; but I know, not too deep down, that I truly desire a first-hand experience of the Barren Grounds.

The Thelon River is part of the Canadian Heritage Rivers System.

VISIONS NORTH

Tuesday, June 22

On Sunday, a nagging feeling resurfaced. For several months I had been mildly concerned that our canoe's centre thwart/carrying yoke might need some repair. I had always assumed, though, that the bolts securing the thwart to the gunwale had merely loosened—that I would need only to tighten the bolts. On inspection, however, the wood through which the bolts passed had nearly rotted away. The yoke would have failed on the first portage!

On Monday morning, 9:00 am, I placed an anxious call to the canoe store. "Do you stock carrying yokes for Mad River Canoes?"

"I'll ask," came the reply from someone who didn't seem to know what a carrying yoke was. Five hours, or perhaps only five minutes later, the tentative voice returned with news that one carrying yoke was available. Ninety-six minutes later the yoke rested snugly in place on our canoe.

This morning, as usual for the past week, I arose at 5:30 am. I wrote another letter of reference, modified my instructions for the Kenyan graduate students arriving in August, and e-mailed the information to the appropriate people.

At 7:00 am, I finished pruning the peonies in a hail storm, and by 8:00, had completed packing our van. At 9:15 Kathleen and I drove into a late June downpour for which Vancouver is so infamous. Even at this late morning hour, commuters jammed both directions of the Trans Canada highway. It seemed an incongruous beginning to a northern Canadian wilderness canoe trip.

Perhaps because of the gloomy, wet weather, we rolled silently for the first hour. After a brief stop at Western Canoeing in Abbotsford to procure a wide-brimmed hat (hopefully our last purchase!), the words came slowly.

"I wonder why we're so nervous and anxious. It's just another canoe trip, like so many canoe and wilderness trips before."

The answer was obvious to both of us. So many unknowns lay before us. We had never been in the wilderness for six weeks. We had never been to the Barren Grounds. We had no feel, no knowledgeable intuition of what to expect. Like all cautious people, therefore, our thoughts dwelled on what could go wrong. We could easily and quickly visualize potential obstacles common to all wilderness canoe trips: wind, rain, bugs, rapids and portages. Yet, we could not visualize any of the positive aspects of canoeing for six weeks on the Barren Grounds. We were depressed.

"Why are we going?" Well, we wanted to share an adventure together, to know our strengths, to build our collective understanding of our relationship. We wanted to see the tundra and its lakes, plants, and animals. We wanted to canoe to Baker Lake. Certainly we would accomplish all these goals. Nonetheless, the unknowns still dominated our thoughts.

For lunch we stopped at the Skihist picnic area, our usual first-day rest-stop on any driving trip into British Columbia's interior. Perched above the Thompson River, enjoying a beer in the sunshine, I felt relaxed. In the evening, camped at our usual first-night stop at Blue Lake, 20 km north of Williams Lake, familiar routines began to assert themselves. We began to enjoy the knowledge that we were actually going to the Thelon River.

Blue Lake, British Columbia

The day is ending with familiar routines: camping in the van; barbecued Bavarian Smokies; cool beer; relaxing in the quiet, fresh air. Despite these pleasures, the apprehension that filled the day remains. Today's quiet, leisurely drive through southern B.C. gave me too much time to think. Our modern civilization, which surrounds us even here at Blue Lake, seems to offer the only certain source of life-sustaining support. For 6 weeks, though, Michael and I will be completely alone. Our safety will depend on our strengths only.

I sit around the campfire, and read again about the European attitude toward the unending distances of the Canadian land mass north of tree line:

> *"It is a land uncircumscribed, for it has no limits that the eye can find. It seems to reach beyond the finite boundaries of this earth. Brooding, immutable, it showed so harsh a face to the first white men who came upon its verges that they named it, in awe and fear, the Barren Grounds."*

So wrote Farley Mowat, in his book Tundra. *Can two people on their own in such a wilderness really safely tend to all their needs? Michael and I are luckier than most people. We have a chance to try.*

Perhaps it's the beer, but I'm starting to relax and feel the excitement. I remember the long winter of preparation, when we dreamed of the challenges of testing ourselves as individuals, and as a couple. Relying on each other, without external intrusions, we can become true partners. The personal potential of such a relationship excites me.

Wednesday, June 23 - Moberly Lake, British Columbia

The splatter of rain on the van this morning shattered my calm resolve of last night. We know so little about the area in which we will spend our entire summer. Our closest personal experience lies approximately 800 km west of the Thelon put-in.

The Northwest Territories' brief profile of the Thelon River describes the portages as "arduous" and "excruciating." Accounts of Barren Grounds trips recount intense rain storms, mid-summer ice-bound lakes that make canoe passage impossible, and tents shredded by the unrelenting wind. What will the weather be like for us this summer? Even on this familiar highway, rain heightens my anxiety.

Because of the rain, we left Blue Lake this morning without breakfast. Driving all day in a grey drizzle, I sensed that both of us were becoming happier and less anxious with our Thelon journey. Vancouver now seemed very far behind us emotionally as we drove through a very familiar environment of grey-green, dense spruce intermixed with boggy opens. We passed through landscapes still comparatively unaffected by human activities, particularly so if you ignored the light green cutblocks regenerating quickly in response to the temperate precipitation.

We sped along on new highway, and occasionally the old road, certainly no more than 20 years abandoned, approached our smoother, newer concrete. I'm sure that some of the old road sections had been unused for as little as 10 years, yet already they supported grasses and shrubs. In a few years they would be barely visible. In 50 years the old highway would appear to be reclaimed by native forest.

This fact comforted me, as I always imagine what any landscape would have looked like before industrial activity stamped its mark. Tapes played on the stereo. Songs from the '60s and '70s. Joan Baez, Simon & Garfunkle, Dylan, Jackson Brown and Jessie Colin Young. Young's lyrics, presented from a native American perspective, reminded me of why I always seek roadless areas, beyond the reach of noise and artifact.

> "I dreamed I was riding in a South Dakota field.
> The sweetgrass whispered to me as I rode.
> The sun, it was at mid-day.
> It shone hot across my face.
> Our land lay still in grace.
> Yes, a crystal silent place.
> Before you came."

I hope and trust that the Thelon River remains a graceful and silent place.

We are now enjoying dinner at our picnic table at Moberly Lake. Michael erected a tarp, beneath which we sit—snug and dry—protected from the evening rain. My tension concerning bad weather on the Thelon River is beginning to fade. For this trip we purchased new rain gear. We made a canoe spray deck and skirts to keep us dry while paddling. We also bought a new tent specifically designed to withstand strong winds. And surely we will enjoy some pleasant weather during the next 6 weeks. Not all days on the river will bring wind, rain, and cold.

Thursday, June 24

I awoke at 5:30 am, and rose to the song and dance of ravens and crows in the 8-degree morning air. All alone, I started a fire, one of my favorite camp activities. Kindling, axed from the inside of split halves, lay piled on newspaper, beneath a teepee of thin, wood strips. Still wet, the fire required repeated blowing until a bed of coals finally produced a sudden, small inferno. With a great deal of satisfaction, sipping a cup of tea, I sat in front of a fire well-made. Kathleen arose two hours later.

Waking to a beautiful calm day, we took our time breaking camp. Michael made bacon, eggs and tea for breakfast, and even did the dishes. I strolled around the camp, with time to botanize and bird watch. Next to the roadside, I identified the small, white Canadian violet. Following a leisurely breakfast, we ambled though the campground with binoculars in hand. After 20 minutes of patience and perseverance, we were rewarded with a magnolia warbler—the first time we had ever seen this summer resident of northern, coniferous forests.

The day's drive was slow. Heading east, we climbed above the spruce into the rolling uplands of the Peace River. Fescue seed and yellow canola—interspersed with strands and splotches of aspen. The region is vast, yet somehow unappealing in its utility and organized network of roads jutting perpendicularly every mile from the highway.

Twin Lakes, Alberta

On the highway, we occasionally stopped for a few last provisions— at Dawson Creek for propane, and at Grimshaw for gas. All-in-all, a pleasant day. During dinner, we encountered our first irritating swarm of mosquitoes. A smudge fire, a walk to the open lake, and a quick retreat to the van completes our day. I hope the bugs on the Thelon River are not incessant.

Knowing what to expect gives me great comfort; the unknown is very intimidating. With 42 unknown days stretching ahead, seemingly without limit, I might have no peace-of-mind. Today we entered new territory; however, the time spent watching birds and looking at plants reminds me that much is familiar. The Thelon River will probably be the same. I need to allow each day to be a new adventure—new places, new birds, and new plants. I will strive to "live for today."

Friday, June 25

Up at 6:30 am, an hour later than usual for the last few weeks, but probably only because our clocks are now on Mountain Time. I set busy tasks for myself around the morning camp while Kathleen slept. I prepared and stacked all the morning firewood. Kathleen slept. I made tea and started the fire. Kathleen slept. I set out all breakfast materials. Kathleen slept.

It's unfortunate that our internal alarms are three hours apart. I try to be patient, as she deserves to awake on her own time. I looked for bread in the Van, shutting the door quietly, but firmly. Kathleen slept.

I paced. Didn't we have to leave by 9:00 am? Already it was 7:30! At ten minutes to 8:00, I couldn't wait. Opening the door, I announced, ever so politely, that it was nearly 8:00.

On the road, northern Alberta views were mainly large tracts of forest broken for agriculture. The road stretched infinitely—and straight—into the horizon. It reminded me of the last night of our Nahanni River trip in 1990. We had left Kraus Hot Springs in the morning. At the end of the day, nearly 100 km later, on the Liard River, we peered into the darkness, searching for the takeout at Blackstone Landing. Paddling into twilight, we were seemingly transfixed in a photograph, moving, but always remaining in place.

Kathleen and I continued to drive north into the unchanging Alberta landscape that stretched before us. Finally, beyond the town of High Level, spruce began to reassert its natural dominance. Deer and black bear became more frequent. Robins, red-winged blackbirds and flickers darted across the road, seemingly playing a dangerous game of avian automobile tag. Frost heaves swelled the pavement— signs of deep, northern frosts.

Twin Falls Park, Northwest Territories

We arrived at the NWT border, and stopped at the tourist centre to acquire maps and information. A canoeing brochure summarized the hardships and necessary precautions of northern water travel. All these things we knew, but the fear of uncertainty struck again. We talked of our misgivings at Louise Falls, where voyageurs must certainly have cursed their three successive portages around deep canyons on the Hay River. We were going to the Thelon River for an adventure—our adventure, shared with no one but ourselves. We might even enjoy

The open tundra provides easy walking and portaging.

Preparing another fantastic breakfast of Lake Trout.

the trip, we reassured ourselves. At times, I think we actually believed we might even have fun. Regardless of any potential struggles, however, we would certainly return to Vancouver, our mutual and personal heroes.

Twin Falls Park contains two spectacular falls: Louise and Alexandra. A short driving day gave us time to explore the park, and to hike along the trail that skirted the canyon wall. The sound of the river was both calming and exciting. Vancouver, and our lives there, now seems very far away.

Along the trail between Louise and Alexandra Falls, we encountered our first horde of northern mosquitoes. We tested various methods of dealing with these bugs, from ignoring them to completely covering ourselves with clothing. Mosquito repellent and covering up afforded the best protection. Nothing stops their incessant, annoying humming. I suppose our patience will be tried severely over the next several weeks.

This afternoon, we picked up some new information packets at the 60th-parallel information centre, operated by the Northwest Territories government. One of these brochures expounded on the dangers of canoeing wilderness rivers in the NWT, which immediately re-awakened my carefully buried worries. With more careful consideration, though, I actually become reassured. Our trip plan already included all the brochure's suggestions such as bringing appropriate gear, allowing adequate time, and allocating a few layover days for bad weather. We can relax tonight, knowing we are finally in the north, and that we are adequately prepared for our journey.

Saturday, June 26; Fort Smith, Northwest Territories

After five days of driving, we're finally here. Fort Smith. Sixty degrees north, on the Alberta-NWT border. Leaving Vancouver in the driving rain last Tuesday morning seems so distant. Blue Lake, Moberly Lake, Twin Lakes, Twin Falls. All points on a mental line to Fort Smith.

After 18 months of planning and preparing, we are finally here. Fort Smith. Our departure terminus. The road from Hay River, 280 flat kilometres through Wood Buffalo National Park, contained no services or population centres. Just featureless boreal forest—a mosaic of spruce and extensive stands of jack pine regenerating after fire. The van contained all that we would need for six weeks on the river: food, clothing, fuel, repair items, first aid kit. We dawdled on the highway, stopping to identify roadside flowers, dominated by a magenta paintbrush. We were relaxed and ready to go.

At the Fort Smith municipal campground, we sat in the warm sunshine and enjoyed a breeze just strong enough to keep the bugs at bay. Nearly idyllic, and similar, we believed, to what we would encounter at Lynx Lake. We were eager to begin our trip, and agreed we probably would be blessed with at least a few days of comfort and ease. Certainly, not all days on the river would bring struggle and fatigue.

Ever since the age of 15, I have longed to live in the wilderness—to breathe, hear and see its natural, seasonal rhythms. I am now poised on the brink of that opportunity. Throughout the day at Fort Smith, I drove very slowly on the loose, gravel roads—not wanting to risk a sudden loss of steering that might send us into the ditch. I stored all river essentials in the locked van whenever away from camp, even for five minutes. I couldn't bear to have anything snatch the Thelon River from me, when so close to the actual event. After 30 years of dreaming, I'm finally here.

Arriving at the terminus of our driving trip, in the warmth of the early afternoon, we visited the Fort Smith information centre to ask directions to the float plane dock. The receptionist informed us that Michael's contact at Loon Air was killed in a crash while testing a new plane just two weeks ago. Another small crack in my carefully-developed armor against worry. A visit to Loon Air confirmed our flight at 8:00 am Monday morning.

After lunch, I easily found the Catholic Cathedral in the centre of Fort Smith. This community seems surprisingly small to support a Cathedral; pews fill only half the church. When Fort Smith became the centre of transportation, at the north end of the historic portage trail from Fort Fitzgerald, its citizens expected that "Smith" would become the territorial capital. The Catholic Church naturally placed their cathedral in Fort Smith. Tomorrow's mass will not be celebrated in the cathedral, however. The scheduling of the annual parish picnic in our campground couldn't have been more convenient for me.

As I rest in our camp, enjoying the evening twilight, my worries about the trip are all but forgotten. Over the last 5 days, the rush and anxiety of Vancouver have been replaced with the calmer rhythms of nature. We've dealt with bugs and rain, encountered animals, and slept with the sound of rivers in our ears. Although we are 350 km from Lynx Lake, I feel I am now in the country where we will live for 6 weeks. The unknown has become the expected.

Sunday, June 27

A slow, relaxing morning. Up at 8:15 am. While Kathleen attended church, I puttered, packed, and strolled to the Slave River viewpoint to bird-watch.

After church, we checked into the hotel for our last night in civilization. Following a lunch of our diminished supply of highway food, we walked down to the Slave River, and spent an hour with the white pelicans in the Rapids of the Drowned. The birds were marvelously acrobatic, like a trained, synchronized swimming team, thrusting their heads forward and down in the water, in perfect unison, searching for fish. Very relaxing for our last afternoon before the Thelon River.

We then visited the museum, bought postcards at the Northern Store, and left our river itinerary with the RCMP.

We wandered back to the hotel, and leisurely spread out all our gear to assess for the last time if we had remembered all the essentials. Item locations were carefully noted as we returned them to the packs. We placed everything neatly in the van, and felt contented and ready.

A few minutes later, the phone rang, ever so lightly and innocently.

"Hello Kathleen, this is Terry. I'd like to speak to Michael."

I knew something was wrong. Neither of us could have guessed that ice would be blocking the outlet of Lynx Lake, and that we couldn't fly in tomorrow as planned. The strong south wind we have experienced in Fort Smith has blown the ice across Lynx Lake, clogging the outlet to the Thelon River. A Loon Air pilot plans to check the ice again tomorrow. If the wind shifts, we should be able to fly in by Tuesday. If not, it might take several days of continued strong, south winds to break up the ice against the north shore.

Extreme disappointment. Oh well, we shrugged. It's just part of a northern trip. What shall we do? Would we put in lower on the River? How long can we delay and still begin at Lynx Lake to paddle the entire Thelon? After a reasoned discussion, we agreed that we must fly in somewhere on the River by Thursday. If Lynx Lake is open by then, we could probably make up the time. We could forego our first rest day at Lynx Lake. We could forego our day in Baker Lake, and we could probably paddle from Aleksektok Rapids to Baker Lake in two, rather than three days. If Lynx Lake remained ice-bound on Thursday, we could simply start farther down the river. We would miss several portages, and still have a great trip. Satisfied with our revised plans, and feeling only slightly frustrated, we made reservations for dinner at a nearby restaurant.

Disappointed, we walked to the Pelican restaurant for dinner. The Chinese restaurant owners, from Vancouver, prepared a great pizza. Our waiter took our minds off our wind-delay problems with questions about life and recent events in Vancouver. He arrived in Fort Smith two years ago to help his brother-in-law and sister, originally planning to stay for only a few months.

Despite the discouraging news of ice on Lynx Lake, our day in Fort Smith had been pleasurable. The town's inviting, friendly atmosphere allayed most of my fears about our canoe trip. We visited the Wood Buffalo National Park information centre, where we saw a multi-projector slide show that heightened my interest in returning someday for a vacation in the Park. Best of all, though, morning Mass—celebrated outside, under the trees—represented a fitting way to embark on my wilderness adventure. The recessional hymn 'Be Not Afraid' reinforced my growing calm.

Monday, June 28

We breakfasted, and renewed our discussion of revised plans. Can we really afford to start three days late? We inspected our itinerary, and agreed we could. Besides, why worry about something that hasn't happened? We may still fly in tomorrow. Heck, we could even still go today, and be right on time!

We checked out of our hotel room, and drove slowly south of town to Loon Air on Four-Mile Lake.

"Any chance of going today?"

"Maybe," Terry replied. "Don is out now, and will be back by noon to let us know."

We waited, chatted about flying and the north, but were reconciled to returning to the municipal campground to hope for the best tomorrow. The radio phone crackled.

"Lynx Lake is open."

"Hey, you're going today," confirmed Terry.

Suddenly, I didn't want to go today. Anxiety resurfaced. I had been looking forward to a shower and barbecued smokies. Hurriedly, we donned our tundra clothes, and trundled our gear to the float dock. The piles were small, but I knew that our gear, canoe, Kathleen and I weighed 640 pounds *(290 kg)*—40 pounds *(18 kg)* more than permitted. Don noted casually that we "seemed to have a lot of stuff."

"I don't see how larger people could stay under 600 pounds *(272 kg)*," I commented.

"They would never get off the water," replied Don.

We taxied to the end of the Lake and began our run into the south wind. I expected the plane to lift by the time we came even with the dock. As we passed by, I thought of blurting out my lie about being exactly at 600 lbs, but kept quiet. We continued down the lake.

"Lift up, lift up, lift up," I thought. I looked at Don. He didn't seem worried. We continued down the lake.

"Lift up, lift up, lift up," I pleaded silently. Don still appeared unworried.

We finally lifted at the lake margin, and banked unsteadily into the wind, seemingly headed to the ground. I continued to sweat for 30 minutes, and felt sick for the entire two-and-one-half hour flight to Lynx Lake.

Lynx Lake

We arrived at Lynx Lake only a few hours later than originally planned. We spent the morning at Loon Air waiting for news of the ice. Watching all of the activity surrounding the float-plane base provided a very interesting morning. Within minutes after our arrival, we helped an independent pilot (Stan) load double-pane windows to be delivered by air to a fishing resort. Stan was proudly flying a Norseman built in 1939, one of only 17 still in service today. The Loon Air people were continually busy flying gas, produce and people throughout the region.

Suddenly, as we were eating lunch, our pilot, Don, arrived.

"I can land you at the Thelon this afternoon."

After a flurry of activity, everything was loaded in the plane, and we double-checked and locked the van. In the rear of the plane, I lay comfortably on top of our gear. The orange I intended to eat on the way to Lynx Lake didn't seem too appealing. I stuffed it into one our white buckets.

Our first view of Lynx Lake showed ice stretching before us as far as we could see. Fortunately, the wind had shifted to blow from the north, and the ice lay pressed against the south shore. Lynx is a beautiful lake. The sun continues to shine at 11:00 pm, and everything is absolutely still. The chirping of Lapland longspurs and Harris' sparrows is barely audible above a background of humming mosquitoes. Soon after landing, we wore our bug jackets, and I expect they will be a constant part of our wardrobe.

I expected to feel a bit of panic as Don flew away. Instead, I wished he had left sooner. I was wishing he would leave us alone, so that we could really begin our great adventure. I feel very calm here, and am trying to enjoy this moment without worrying about tomorrow. All wilderness canoe trips include separation from civilization that signifies a new beginning. Our adventure is now beginning; its story and its ending remain unknown.

I'm very happy to be at Lynx Lake. Kathleen and I have taken two tundra walks, have dined on soup and gorp, have enjoyed a profusion of blooming alpine azaleas, and are writing in our journals beneath the bright 11:00 pm sun. A Pacific loon wails across the lake. I'm very happy to be here.

Ever since I first back-packed into the wilderness as a young boy, I've dreamed of walking down the trail and never having to return. The ultimate fantasy of living free. Wilderness canoeing is as close as I'll ever come to this romantic ideal. Tomorrow morning, Kathleen and I will glide across this calm bay at the eastern edge of Lynx Lake. We will paddle effortlessly through the outlet to be swept away by the Thelon River, not only to challenge our fears of the unknown, but also to embrace our romantic fantasies of wilderness travel.

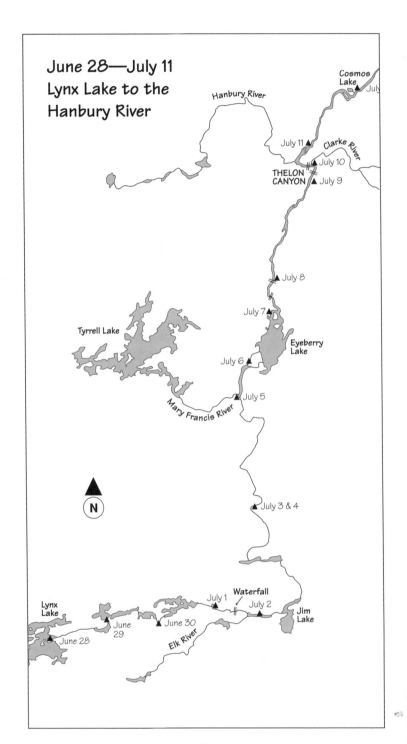

June 28—July 11
Lynx Lake to the
Hanbury River

Hanbury River

Cosmos Lake
July

July 11
Clarke River
July 10
THELON CANYON
July 9

July 8

July 7

Tyrrell Lake

Eyeberry Lake

July 6

July 5

Mary Francis River

N

July 3 & 4

Waterfall

Lynx Lake

July 1
July 2

Jim Lake

June 29
June 30

Elk River

June 28

SEPARATION

Tuesday, June 29

We're sitting in our tent, having completed only 20 of the 30 km planned for today. Although beautiful, the river presents the worst of all possible paddling combinations: strong winds, no current and long, wide, flat, lake-like sections separated by short, turbulent rapids, one of which required portaging. The maps indicate we may need to endure as many as three portages tomorrow.

One of the rapids today coursed through a very narrow outlet hidden in one of the many bays lining the river. Although Kathleen and I scanned the bay with binoculars, a short peninsula obscured the outlet from our view. We paddled about two hours searching the next bay before returning to where we suspected the outlet must be.

We're camped again on a sandy beach. Our door faces to view the northern horizon, across which the sun slides east to the new dawn without ever fully relinquishing the day. Only 30

metres away, a common loon swims and yodels joyfully, directly opposite our tent door. Canada geese gabble along the shore.
We are alone in our Barren Grounds—tired, but content.

Wednesday, June 30

Ten-thirty pm. In the tent. A very long day. The maps fail to
indicate adequately that the Thelon River is actually a lake,
punctuated by short bursts of impassable rapids. Two portages
today, the second requiring about 2.5 hours over boggy, buggy
terrain. At least one, possibly three more portages wait for us
tomorrow. We're beginning to feel tired, and are already about
25 km behind schedule after only two days on the river. On the
positive side of the ledger, we have completed as many
portages as we had intended by this evening's camp.

Our spirits remain high, and I'm particularly impressed
with how well Kathleen perseveres throughout all these unex-
pected difficulties. Her continued positive attitude makes it
easier for me to remain optimistic.

*Other than being tired, and behind our itinerary, I am glad to
be here. Beautiful scenery and afternoon temperatures in the high
twenties make the land more hospitable than I expected. If the current would only quicken, our hours on the river would decrease, and
we would have more time for relaxing and enjoying the tundra birds
and plants.*

*These first two days have been long and tiring. I expected a fast-
flowing river, down which we could simply float. Instead, the wide,
flat stretches encountered so far provide no current. Changes in river
elevation and gradients come abruptly, and create un-runnable rapids.
Three portages are behind us. We expect two more tomorrow. Our
longest portage today equalled only one kilometre. Such apparent distances, however, are deceptive. Even though only one kilometre was
indicated on the map, Michael and I both carried four loads to the end
of the rapid, for a total of 7 km each. Fortunately, the open terrain of
the riverside tundra affords easy walking.*

Winter has barely left this land. Snow lies on our campsite beach. Just over the ridge behind camp, a large chunk of ice melts slowly. Because we both felt so stuffed after last night's meal, I cooked only a portion of tonight's dinner. I'm now confident that we have brought plenty of food for this trip.

Thursday, July 1

The endless sky occupied my thoughts on the river today. Clouds seem to hang motionless, as though suspended from the very ceiling of the heavens. Rainstorms are easily visible, even though they usually remain many kilometres distant.

A map is essential in this flat, limitless tundra. With little or no current, we have difficulty finding the right route down this wide river, with its many deep bays. Today, we paddled around a bend toward some trees growing in the center of the channel. As we aligned the boat with the current to drift by the small islands, we seemed to be slipping backwards. The strong head winds and waves affected our ability to read the current properly. After a few more attempts, we realized that we were actually paddling up stream on a side channel of the Thelon!

We carried our four loads of gear around another long rapid today. Portaging allows time on the land, where the colourful flowers of miniature plants, such as alpine azalea, are just beginning to bloom. This floral display lifts my spirits as I trudge beneath heavy loads. We have become discouraged having to portage nearly every stretch of rapidly-moving water, although we did run one rapid today. The river also began to flow a little more quickly, and we made good progress, even into a strong head wind.

I wore my bug hat for the first time today. Although stuffy, and hard to see through, the netting brought welcome relief when the swarms of mosquitoes became unbearable.

Another difficult day. On the river at 8:45 am—off at 6:15 pm. We struggled against head winds all day. We remain 25 km behind schedule, and failed to even reach the reportedly "grueling" portage listed on today's itinerary.

The wind makes life tense. We paddled beneath overcast skies, and the temperatures reached only 17 degrees compared to 20-21 for the last few days. Quite cool, but fewer bugs. We've camped on very open tundra this evening. Thank goodness we brought our backpacking stove, as no wood is available for cooking fires.

The Barren Grounds stretch infinitely flat, and the river offers many large side bays to fool the unwary pathfinder. There have been highlights today, however. The horizon filled with clouds and light/dark patterns that cloaked distant rain showers. Arctic terns hovered and plunged into the water, submerging themselves head-first in pursuit of fish. At the end of the paddling day, we saw our first caribou, and after dinner we were able to strip and wash, as the winds kept all mosquitoes cowering at ground level. I hope that tomorrow's portage isn't too difficult, and that we don't fall much farther behind our schedule. I would be disappointed to use any of our planned rest days for travel, as we haven't had any time yet for plants, birds and leisurely tundra hikes.

Friday, July 2

We're in the tent at 9:30 pm. The winds are finally abating slightly after blowing steadily for nearly 48 hours. We were driven to shore early today by the wind on a "lake" section of the river below the confluence with the Elk River. The canoe was being blown backwards, and waves began breaking over our bow, as we braced against the metre-high rollers.

Despite the wind, however, it's been a good day. The portage, although the lengthiest so far, wasn't as grueling as promised. We began packing our gear along the edge of the canyon before noon, when we were still comparatively fresh and strong.

After lunch, capped with a reward of juicy, greasy, vacuum-packed sausage, we strolled back along the canyon ridge to photograph plants, such as alpine azalea, which were just now coming into full spring bloom. We then returned for one last look at the falls, which, surprisingly, are un-named on the topographic map. Standing above the precipice, the cataract's power and grandeur swept over me, similar to my feelings at Virginia Falls on the Nahanni River three years earlier. Although not rivalling the height of Virginia Falls, the sudden, multi-channeled maelstrom before me created an impressive transition to the low Arctic plain extending to the East.

Below the falls and its outlet rapid, the river finally offered quick-flowing, runnable white-water. My confidence grew with each rock dodged, with each ferry executed properly, and with each eddy hit high. Kathleen performed very well, controlling the back-ferries and reading the flow of water to avoid rocks and souse holes. Although my mouth dried on several occasions, I'm beginning to think we won't need to portage all rapids before the Hanbury junction.

During these first days on the river, I have felt somewhat intimidated, even by grade 2 water. I think I feel personally responsible for our success or failure. I worry that a dumping, which can occur even with a trivial mistake, could be fatal in these cold waters. At best, a capsize would likely be the end of our adventure. I sense that Kathleen is somewhat disappointed with my timidity.

At camp, we climbed a low knoll, and were rewarded with endless vistas of horizon, tundra, and innumerable lakes and water flowing seemingly everywhere. In all this space, we are the only humans. We have seen no people, have heard no planes, and only on a portage trail did we notice signs of previous human activity: one glove and shards of mosquito netting. The Thelon River drains a vast region populated primarily by animals, functioning as it has since the ice receded 8,000 years ago. I'm feeling content, even though we have now fallen 55 km behind schedule.

After a tough paddling day, we camped sooner than planned, as the rising wind forced us from the water at 5:00 pm. The wind has blown steadily for the last two days; strong enough last night to cause me to worry about the tent holding up. I feel vulnerable with no relief in the terrain to protect us from the wind.

Today brought another portage, the longest of the trip so far— "1.2 km over some pretty rough country," according to the NWT guide. Although the map clearly indicates a waterfall, I didn't expect the falls to be so spectacular after travelling through such low country. Almost as soon as we heard the roar of cascading water, we left the canoe to scout along the ridge. Michael and I tend to be cautious, and assumed we would eventually be able to paddle closer to the falls before beginning our portage. There were no more chances to eddy out, however, which justified our prudence.

Canada geese have become our constant companions. Again, today, we saw hundreds. I'm still fooled by large groups of "animals" running up the riverbanks, only to realize the animals are actually molting geese fleeing by foot, their only means of escape. The geese have revealed many of their summer secrets on this river, and I very much enjoy their company.

Wind also provides constant companionship, although its threatening, pervasive presence brings far less pleasure than does my new friendship with the geese. Before the portage around the falls, we paddled two hours directly into an unceasing head wind. Back on the river below the outlet rapids, we encountered some quite challenging white water, made even more so by the strong, wind-generated waves. It was difficult to distinguish the waves caused by wind from those caused by rocks, adding tension to running the rock garden.

Although our evening camp spot was again forced upon us by the wind, we found a sheltered place for the tent above a smooth, sandy beach. We are protected from the strongest winds, yet are still mostly mosquito-free. We even took off our clothes and sponge-bathed in the warm sun.

Our first food "disaster" nearly occurred today; the white bucket containing the gorp wasn't closed properly, allowing water to leak in. All but two packages, though, were completely recoverable.

Before burning the water-soaked clumps of lumpy gorp, Michael patiently retrieved and ate every licorice allsort.

Saturday, July 3

We spent a long day of contrasting emotions: satisfaction, calmness, accomplishment and utter fatigue. The day began warm and calm, which allowed us to complete a long, lake-like section of the river at approximately 4 km/hour. Our best flat-water pace yet! The river then narrowed and quickened, easily carrying us 12 more kilometres until we stopped for lunch at 12:30. We were pleased with the ease of our progress, and chattered confidently about being able to gain on our arbitrary, but ill-informed schedule.

Twenty minutes after lunch, we approached the narrow outlet of Jim Lake, beached our canoe and climbed the low bank to have a look. Jim Lake is a large expanse of water, certainly much larger than any of the lakes we had previously traversed. We shared relief that the Thelon didn't force us through Jim Lake's cold north-western bay, still jammed with ice pushed there by the last two days of constant south-east winds.

After Jim Lake, the Thelon finally became a river, transporting us 12 km in slightly more than one hour. A joyful time of care-free canoeing on a sparkling river with no hazards. Such exhilaration embodies one of the major joys of canoeing!

The river then emptied and turned into a 12-km, west-flowing "lake," the last large body of flatwater before Eyeberry Lake. We now enjoyed a tail wind, but dismissed the idea of hoisting our sail as too much trouble. I soon realized, however, that by angling the canoe slightly broadside to the wind, the effect of sailing could be reasonably approximated. We covered nearly half the "lake's" distance in only 45 minutes. This was wonderful. We really were gaining on our schedule!

At a narrows in the "lake," in a bay on the north shore, we saw a cabin and several outbuildings, our first indication that other people inhabited our region. We chose not to cross the open water for a visit.

We did, however, decide to cross immediately after the narrows, as the Thelon flowed out from the north side of the "lake." We had been "sailing" and paddling very comfortably, protected from the southeast wind in the lee of the south shore. We reasoned, however, that we should cross to the north shore now, rather than risk a larger crossing opposite the outlet.

As soon as we reached the north shore, winds and rolling waves bounced and tossed the canoe. Whenever the south shore veered away, the waves became larger as they gained momentum across this lake-like section of the river. The conditions reached the limit of our comfort, skill and strength. We continued to struggle, though, as we very much wanted to be off these flat-water sections of the Thelon River. We longed to wake the next morning on a flowing river, free of threats from latent, lurking head winds and breaking waves.

Ninety minutes later, we turned north onto the flowing Thelon River into a world of quiet, light, calm, and swiftly-flowing water! Such a complete and instant transition from the wind-blown lake environment. We drifted along, repeatedly entertained by the flightless geese running before us along the riverbanks. At 6:00 pm we agreed to camp at the first suitable, riverside spot, preferably one with a sandbar and grove of trees for shelter and wood. At 7:00 pm, we lowered our expectations, and stopped to assess a gravel slope with dwarf birch, 100 m from the river's edge. In the past hour, we had seen no better camping spots. The Thelon's banks were still lined with large bands of ice, which obviously filled the narrow, high-walled channel, scouring all sand, soil and vegetation with each spring breakup. There was nowhere to camp.

At 9:00 pm, we'd had enough, and were ready to accept any campsite large enough to pitch the tent. We ferried to a small eddy, impatiently lugged our gear up a 10-m boulder-strewn embankment, and set up camp. By 10:30 we had dined on beef jerky stew, and are now lying in the tent, sipping tea. It had actually been a very good day. No portages, and we had travelled 60-70 km, nearly as far as the first four days combined. We were only 20 km behind schedule, and only 40-50 km from the Mary Francis River, a distance we should be able to gain in one day. We decided to sleep in, and take our rest day one day early. We are camped on open, flat tundra, which should provide good hiking and bird-watching.

Of all that happened today, though, I was most impressed with Kathleen. Coming straight from her Vancouver office, she has calmly endured grueling portages, innumerable swarming bugs, threatening rapids, vindictive winds, and very long days. Despite all these obstacles, Kathleen perseveres with enthusiasm and grace; she was truly spectacular in the way she paddled, without complaint, for nearly 12 hours, despite her frustration and physical fatigue. I can't imagine sharing this adventure with anyone other than Kathleen.

Sunday, July 4

Our 12th wedding anniversary. A very appropriate and relaxing rest day. We awoke at 9:00 am, and I surprised Kathleen with a card, and a pair of silver, west-coast Indian earrings. The card had successfully hidden from her discovery in the first aid kit, even though she opened the kit daily. Kathleen was quite touched. I did well.

I then made tea, and approached the river to try to catch a grayling or two for breakfast. The Arctic grayling may be the world's most perfect fish for canoeists: easy to catch, just the right size to fit in the pan, and very tasty. After the 10th unsuccessful cast, I decided to return to camp to prepare our usual bannock. Turning toward the bank, I saw Kathleen with the camera. I decided to cast a few more times for the photographic pose. On the third attempt, I hooked a gigantic fish! After 15 minutes and three runs, the 78-cm lake trout lay on the rocky beach.

In the afternoon, we strolled casually across the tundra—limitless, generally featureless, and repetitious in its mix of plants: bog Rosemary, bog laurel, red bearberry, dwarf birch, northern Labrador tea, cloud berry, crowberry and lichens. The spaciousness seemed empty of large animals.

Back at camp, Kathleen read, while I napped and replaced a broken snap on the spray deck. I played at erecting a tarp for shade, but the wind proved superior to all knots, bracings and angles. I finally succeeded, or the wind stopped playing, at 8:30 pm. We wrote in our diaries behind the tarp's shade.

Tomorrow our goal is the Mary Francis River—45 km to be back on schedule. Twelve km of rock gardens. But that's tomorrow. Tonight we head to the tent for anniversary brandy.

After yesterday's 12-hour, 70-km paddle, I'm appreciating our first layover day of the trip. Last night we kept paddling, looking for a river-level, dry, unexposed campsite. Such sites don't exist in this part of the country, as the river is constrained by high banks. Although not a sandy beach, we are happy with this lovely tundra camp on a ridge with a view high above the river. We had hoped that being so exposed to the wind would cut down on the bugs, but they continue to torment us in hordes that surpass anything we have seen so far.

I awoke this morning to find a card and present on my pillow. My thoughtful husband Michael had carried them in places I looked every day: the card in the first aid case; earrings in a box in the toiletry case. I must be blind. As usual, Michael wrote a beautiful inscription that made me feel so special and loved.

We enjoyed a pleasant rest day just taking it easy. Michael fished and I retrieved the camera to capture our anniversary camp on film. I anticipated a perfect picture, with snow and ice on the opposite bank, and Michael fishing in the foreground. My hopes were ruined when Michael walked away from the shore. Seeing me peering through the lens, however, he cast again to allow me to get my picture. As the shutter clicked, Michael called out that he had a "giant fish." I helped guide the fish into the small net, which barely contained half the fish's length. We estimated the lake trout's weight at about 8 kg. We enjoyed a delicious breakfast, and expect to have many more meals from this trout.

We tried to erect our tarp today, not because of rain, but to obtain relief from the 28-degree sun that never seems to fully set. The strong, tundra winds flattened the tarp on every attempt. We continued to bake in the unceasing sun, and I retreated to the tent for shade. Cut off from the cooling winds of the open tundra, I felt even hotter than before. Even so, I preferred to hide in the stuffy tent, rather than endure the direct rays of the afternoon sun.

Reading excerpts from Edgar Christian's journal Unflinching, I was impressed with the perseverance of Hornby, Adlard, and Christian in the face of so much hardship. These 3 men entered the Thelon Region during the winter of 1926-27, and intended to live off caribou while they trapped for furs. Unfortunately, Hornby, Adlard, and Christian arrived too late, as the vast herds had already migrated south; all 3 men subsequently starved to death. Only 19 years old when he died, Christian survived until June, and succumbed just 3 weeks before the Arctic spring returned; his diary makes compelling reading regarding the extraordinary endurance of which the human spirit is capable, despite what turned out to be insurmountable odds against survival. We hope to be able to find their cabin at Hornby Point, which now lies only a few days down river.

Although this land lacks trees and has little relief, the tundra is by no means barren or uninteresting. There are many varieties of low-growing plants, most just starting to bloom. Today we also saw 3 gulls, a few meadowlarks and one Lapland longspur. Other than mosquitoes, however, geese are the most abundant wildlife.

We had benefited from a light tail wind most of yesterday, but in the afternoon we had paddled away from the southern, lee shore to battle strong winds and high waves for the last few kilometres of the lake-like, 1-km wide section of the Thelon. We knew once we left this open stretch, that the winds wouldn't be able to affect us as much. We continued to stroke hard to reach a narrow section of the river flowing out of the north side of the "lake." It was like heaven

M. Pitt

Lunch opposite white sand esker downstream of Jim Lake.

K. Pitt

Fish for breakfast, lunch, hors d'oeuvres, and dinner.

*when we paddled around the island at the river's exit from our flat-
water, wind-blown, struggle. The island blocked the wind, and the
current flowed quickly. We lay our paddles across the gunwales and
just drifted. Now that the Thelon is moving, we expect to make up
the kilometres lost on the "lakey" part of the trip. We hope to be able
to leave the Mary Francis River, as planned, on July 6.*

*Tomorrow we paddle through a rock garden section that will
require considerable maneuvering. We're worried, but the combination of our river skills and our conservative natures will get us
through safely.*

Monday, July 5

*As befits a day spent running rapids in a rock garden, tonight we are
camped in a rock garden. Rocks are everywhere—large and small,
round and flat. Rocks, just scattered, all around. Although there
didn't appear to be anywhere to place our tent, we are becoming
adept at finding a spot just the right size. We reached the Mary
Francis River about 7:30 pm. Most of the rock garden section was
easy, but a couple of bends proved challenging. The last section con-
sisted of two rock ledges that extended most of the way across the
river. We portaged the first ledge, in a strong wind, which made carrying the canoe very difficult for Michael. After scouting the second
ledge, we decided to ferry to river right, where there appeared to be
more room around the ledge. This river is substantially wider than
those we usually canoe. Ferries are therefore much longer, and must
be initiated well above the obstacles.*

*We finished the fish for dinner, our last of five consecutive trout
meals. Although tasty, I look forward to eating something else for
variety.*

*After making camp, we watched four muskoxen across the
Mary Francis River. They seemed to enjoy butting heads, and shat-
tering the tundra quiet with their noisy impacts.*

What a day. Once again it began in sunshine, with relatively calm conditions. The mosquitoes were as bad as they've
been on the entire trip, but quite tolerable with our bug jackets.

I prepared a leisurely breakfast of lake trout and tea, and we were on the river by 9:20 am, hoping to reach the Mary Francis River before we camped.

The topographic map showed many rocks, particularly in the 12 km before the Mary Francis, a section also indicated in our guide as requiring considerable maneuvering to canoe it safely.

By noon we had covered nearly half the distance, and virtually all of the alleged rocks lay safely submerged below the surface. The current was gaining speed, the sun shone, and a light breeze from the north provided ideal paddling conditions. I felt optimistic and happy.

We stopped for lunch on a gravel embankment, and enjoyed lake trout paté on crackers. Just like having hors d'oeuvres at a cocktail party. I'm bored with eating lake trout all the time, though. Not wanting to keep fresh fish in camp, because of our concern about raids from Barren-Ground grizzlies, we immediately cooked and began eating the trout after catching it yesterday morning. Since then it's been lake trout for breakfast, lake trout for lunch, lake trout for snacks, and lake trout for dinner. These Thelon River fish are too big for canoeists on the move! My fishing pole is now packed away, and I won't be trying to catch any more trout in the near future.

After lunch, we saw our second caribou as we drifted away from the beach. Paddling beneath a warm sun, we continued to excite flightless, nesting Canada geese. Gliding past one low island, we sent a flock of about six splashing simultaneously into the water. As we passed, they realized that safety lay on dry land, and the flock, as one, ran back up the bank into the willows, heads held low in the "sneak" position.

We continued to travel fast, passing more mapped, submerged rocks, and I began to look forward to an early camp, perhaps 5:00 or maybe even 4:00 pm. The map suggested a back-eddy opposite the Mary Francis River that might provide a sandy beach.

By 2:00, the wind quickened, and the rocks sat defiantly above the water, flanked by ledges jutting out from both sides of the river. Scouting became necessary, and the constant vigilance inserted tension into what had been a lackadaisical day.

On most rivers we have run, the safest route generally exists on the inside bend, which usually has slower water flanked by an eddy. Outside bends stack the flowing water in larger, standing waves, and may have sweepers jutting out from undercut banks. On the Thelon, however, inside bends are often the least safe. The shallower water reveals more rocks, and ledges extend further from shore. The outside bend exhibits fewer rocks, and usually provides enough room to avoid the high standing waves.

Not always, however. As we approached the next bend, ledges obviously extended from both banks, nearly meeting in the middle. We beached, and scouted from a low ridge above the chute.

"Heck," I suggested, "all we need to do is line up, and hit the down-stream V."

"Those waves below the ledge are just haystacks."

"We can run this."

We ferried out, headed for the "V," and then noticed for the first time a large rock, hidden behind a flashing wave. We side-slipped right, perilously close to the ledge, avoided the rock, side-slipped left, and hit the "V."

"Oh, my God, these may be just haystacks, but they're awfully big." We braced with all our strength, hoping to exit upright. It seemed we were held in place by the standing waves, forever suspended in the brace position. Would we remain here until freeze-up, at which time we could walk across the haystacks to shore? Eventually we emerged from the white rollers, and congratulated ourselves for having taken the time to wear our spray skirts, stretched water-tight over the cowling of the spray deck.

Only two more ledges before the Mary Francis River and the anticipated white sand beach. We lifted over the first ledge, a short portage of 50 m. We avoided the second ledge by ferrying all the way across the river. At 6:45, a strong north wind blew directly towards us. Why does the wind always shift to meet us at the end of the day, no matter what direction we're travelling?

We arrived at the Mary Francis River at 7:30 pm, with four muskoxen visible on the far shore. The white sand beach of our visions and hopes had rudely metamorphosed into an expanse of large boulders. Too tired to continue, we fitted the tent between rocks as best we could, made a fire, and ate the last of the lake trout.

After dinner, we strolled up the Mary Francis River to view the muskoxen browsing and head-butting. Although we enjoyed their display, I hoped these impressive animals would stay on the far side of the river. We had pitched our tent on their trail, and the adjacent spruce and willows showed obvious signs of muskox rubbing and damage.

Back at camp, as we packed and stowed our gear for the night, the north wind intensified. The tundra bugs that had plagued us continually for the past week fled before the strong gusts. For the first time, we enjoyed sitting outside, lingering, without our bug jackets. It's now midnight, and I'm lying, very tired, in the tent. Our previous extended canoe trip on the Nahanni River was a float compared to this challenging adventure. I hope tomorrow will be a short, easy day.

Tuesday, July 6

Well, I got my wish for a short day. Up at 8:00 am, and on the river at 11:00. Off the river at 3:00 pm. Writing in the tent 2 hours later. I didn't receive my wish for an easy day, however. We awoke to a strong north wind (a head wind, naturally), and a cool 10-degree morning. No bugs. We paddled continuously against the wind. At first, the current proved a strong ally, and we made progress. As the Thelon flattened and braided into a delta before Eyeberry Lake, however, the current abandoned us to struggle alone against the wind. The outcome was never in doubt.

Here we sit in the tent at 5:30 pm, grounded by wind. We're camped on a low, sandy island, on the lee side of a dune. It's warm, calm and comforting out of the wind. Also, still no bugs, for nearly 36 hours now. *We paddled about 16 km of our intended 38 km today, mostly into a head wind that grew continually stronger. The river's shoreline was often broken by large bays, and we were unable to make the open crossings safely. Instead, our only hope was to paddle directly into the teeth of the wind to reach the lee shore at the foot of the bay.*

Entering one particular inlet towards the end of the day, we managed only to barely hold our position against the unceasing wind. Refusing to yield, I muttered defiant challenges to the wind: "This time I will not stop. I will keep paddling no matter how hard you blow!" We managed to push forward slightly, and finally reached the lee of the harbour. As we rested in the relative calm, Michael acknowledged that he had nearly given up, and had been resigned to making camp. I felt proud when he said that only my determination had brought us this victory against our unyielding opponent.

Despite our struggle with the wind, the day provided memorable wildlife highlights, including 12 muskoxen just beyond the Mary Francis River. Just before we stopped for the day, a lone greyish-white wolf approached to within 50 m as we neared each other along the shoreline. As we floated by the wolf, a cow moose and calf leaped from the willows into the water not more than 20 m from the canoe. At that proximity, the cow moose looked menacingly large. *The moose retreated to the bushes, but her calf remained in our path. The wind was so strong that we drifted backwards whenever we stopped stroking hard. We certainly didn't want to lose any of our hard-fought progress. We also didn't want to paddle between a cow moose and her calf, so we ferried across to the island on which we are now camped.*

We intend to nap for a while, get up, eat dinner and return to bed, hoping the wind will diminish in the evening so that we can begin paddling about 3:00 am. Most nights and mornings have been calm, although there have been a couple of nights when the wind didn't ever subside. Wind continuously hinders our progress, and we are very worried about reaching Baker Lake on time. I know my parents will expect to receive a telephone call from us no later than the day of our anticipated arrival; I don't wish to cause them needless anxiety by being late.

We have a nice camp. A sandy, flat spot, and plenty of broken driftwood for a fire. We plan to sleep until the wind dies, get up and cook our chili dinner, and see how close we can get to the Thelon Canyon tomorrow.

After napping until 11:30 pm, we awoke to a lesser breeze. Encouraged, we dressed, enjoyed watching a pair of greater white-fronted geese nesting on a small, nearby pond, built a fire, and dined on chili and cornbread.

After our midnight snack, the wind remained brisk, making the 20-degree temperature seem cold. We discussed our options and retired to the tent, hoping for calmer, warmer conditions in a few hours.

Wednesday, July 7

Up at 6:15 am. The wind blew all night, but has slackened to paddleable conditions. We breakfasted on granola, quickly packed and loaded the canoe, and paddled away an hour later.

Into the wind—8-degrees—it was cold. I had on all my gear: wet suit booties, long underwear, shirt, sweater, windbreaker, touque, hat and neoprene paddling gloves. I felt warm, but not toasty. Even the exertion of paddling against the wind didn't generate excess heat.

We reached Eyeberry Lake at 9:00 am. Perhaps we will have a good day, and put some miles behind us. We could hug the west shore, which would buffer us partly from the now brisk NNW wind.

We rounded the point into the Lake, turned north, and gazed across an ocean stretching before us. We could see no end to Eyeberry Lake—just wind-blown whitecaps rolling toward us from beyond the horizon. Don't think about the destination. It's too daunting. One bay, one point at a time, would get us there. We sneaked down Eyeberry Lake along its 3-m embankment. Comparatively little wind. This will work.

We reached our first bay. Too far across the mouth to traverse in these breakers. We paddled around the point, directly into the wind. Virtually no progress, even though both of us paddled with maximum energy. With each stroke closer to the distant shore, the wind and waves slackened imperceptibly, but assuredly, until we reached the calm, 2-m-high lee shore. Then, broadside to the wind, we sailed down the foot of the bay until we reached the opposite shore and turned out, running before breakers and wind.

"We can do this. This will work. If only that wind would die, damn it!"

By 2:00 pm we had struggled 5 km to the north end of the lake and rode the current through the narrows.

"We win!"

Now we can let the current work for us. Around a bend and into a wide part of the river with a very deep bay extending into the wind. Its opposite shore, only one metre high, offered no wind protection. Rollers piled towards us. We struggled, gained half a canoe length; struggled, gained a quarter canoe length; struggled and lost the battle. Two-thirty. Camp is where your canoe blows to shore.

Tonight's home is a low piece of tundra fringed with dwarf birch, which provides sufficient numbers of small sticks to cook our stir-fry with rice. During dinner, the wind stopped, and innumerable magnitudes of small, mosquito-like bugs rose from the birch-clothed tundra. They didn't bite. They simply rose, and with the first breeze, fell to earth, covering our gear, inundating our packs, and generally making a nuisance of themselves. Better than biting mosquitoes, though.

The wind has not lessened at all for the last 2 days. Yesterday we woke at about midnight to stand on the beach. Even in the lee of our sand dune, we felt oppressed by the wind, which remained too strong to paddle against. We ate dinner and then slept until 6:00 am. Following a quick breakfast, we began paddling into a blustery, grey morning. After travelling only about 15 km, the wind and waves again forced us to shore, and an early camp near the outlet of Eyeberry Lake. The evening is now calm, but we're both tired. We'll go to bed immediately after dinner, get up early, and try again tomorrow.

In the tent at 6:00 pm. The wind has now slackened substantially. If only it stays that way, we can be on the river at 5:00 am. Assuming we can run all the rapids, we will reach the canyon tomorrow afternoon. I hope so, as we're 45 km behind schedule again, even though we're working very hard.

Thursday, July 8

The wind renewed its attack at 2:00 am, reinforced soon after by rain. "A short storm would be fine. We could still be on the water in sunshine and calm by 5:00 am."

The assault continued at 6:00 am. We were warm and dry, though, in our new tent, designed to withstand all but the most extreme weather conditions. The open vestibule at our head provided ample protection even for the boots and daypack stored outside the sleeping area.

We preferred to sleep with both tent doors open, for ventilation and to be able to scan our environment. I peered through the front door at our feet to confirm that canoe, gear and food had remained undisturbed during the night.

"Oh, no!" Rain had been blowing into the tent for the past four hours. My shirt, sweater, bird and plant books, and the bottoms of our sleeping bags lay soaking in tepid water. What a stupid, careless mistake. I hate such mistakes because they're so easily avoided. The clothes and sleeping bags would dry, but the books would never recover completely.

Our bird and plant books comprise a major part of all our wilderness trips. Although we know most of the common plants by sight, books are necessary to recognize species that are new to us. Without our book, we would never have identified the prickly saxifrage, white petals delicately spotted in orange, growing among the riverside cobbles at the Mary Francis River. Without our bird book, we would never have confirmed the greater white-fronted goose in the pond behind last night's camp in the delta south of Eyeberry Lake. The books will still be serviceable. Their crinkled pages may even be viewed with admiration as having "field character," but I don't like it.

Ten o'clock in the morning, and the rain and wind have continued mercilessly for 8 hours. There's still time for a full day of paddling, even if we leave by two or three. It seems, however, that today is becoming a rest day, even if imposed upon us.

It stormed all night and day. We remained in the tent, very dis-couraged with our lack of progress. After breakfast of bannock and tea at 6:00 pm, we loaded the canoe, and set out in a calm breeze. We easily completed the crossing of the bay at the north end of Eyeberry Lake and reached moving water, where the wind began to blow again. We stopped at the first bend to scout a rapid marked on the map. We were both very pensive about the wind. Paddling into the wind is not only hard work, but also risky. On a calm river, rocks identify their positions by creating waves. Additional waves made by wind complicate the difficulty of river-reading. A strong wind also forces additional canoe-alignment adjustments when maneuvering around rocks. While waiting for the wind to die down, we walked the entire length of the river bend. Although the wind never slackened, we eventually decided that we needed to run this stretch of river to gain confidence.

Beyond the bend, the river opened into a wide section, where the wind now blew very strongly. As we paddled through the haystacks into the flat water, a large bay opened up on river-right.

We suddenly found ourselves far from the safety of shore. I was truly scared as we sought to reach the beach, running in silence before the large waves. We stopped about 12:30 am, ate some soup and retired to the tent. Just before we reached camp, the sky had been nearly completely clear. I now looked out at an almost completely cloud-filled sky. The air is quite cool in the low sun and strong wind. Another storm seems to be blowing toward us. I am so frustrated not to be able to make any progress because of poor weather.

I'm now back in the tent, 20 km past last evening's camp at Eyeberry Lake. Two o'clock in the morning. We're both very tired—only a cup of soup for dinner. While still at Eyeberry Lake this morning, we played some cribbage, napped a bit, and then made afternoon tea. At 4:00 pm the wind stopped, and soon the rain also stopped. We make a breakfast bannock, and were on the water at 6:00 pm.

It felt good. No wind. At 6:30, a gentle breeze arose.

"I don't like this."

"It's just a breeze," came Kathleen's response from the bow.

By 7:00 pm, we reached moving water north of Eyeberry Lake, and the wind direction reversed to once again blow directly into our faces. Combined with a fast-flowing current, some rocks, and an approaching rapid, the wind made controlling the canoe difficult. We were off the water at 7:30.

"Oh, well. Time for a tundra hike."

While being harassed incessantly by a peregrine falcon, we strolled very disconsolately down stream, along the cliff, assessing the rapid.

"We could do it easily if it weren't for the wind."

Two hours passed and the gusts grew stronger and more prolonged. For the first time I considered the possibility we would never reach Baker Lake. Maybe we should just run this rapid, wind or no wind.

A few minutes later, Kathleen voiced my thoughts. "Why can't we run this rapid? Is it only because of the wind? It's one thing to be cautious because we're all alone, but we still have to run what we know we can run."

And so, here we are—finally beyond Eyeberry Lake— finally relaxing—finally enjoying a beautiful evening in low-angle sunlight. Only 40 km and one portage behind schedule. The wind is blowing strongly once again, but I'm a happy guy. I believe we will reach Baker Lake on time.

Friday, July 9

Today began windy, following a noisy, turbulent night of what were probably the strongest winds of the trip so far. While fetching water for breakfast, I was attacked by an Arctic tern. Believing I must be near the nest, I closely watched her retreat. She flew to her nest on an exposed, rocky beach. The tern's colouring makes her very diffi-cult to see, even now that I know where she is. The storm last night was fierce; but, this little bird sits on her nest without any protection from the Arctic winds.

The wind blew very strongly all night, stronger than at any other time on the trip. The noise interrupted our fitful and restless sleep. I'm just glad the tent withstood the unceasing gusts.

We arose at 11:00 am, and found a sheltered spot behind a willow-clothed sand dune to cook a spaghetti breakfast, a meal originally intended for last night's dinner. The sheltered "kitchen" was quiet—so nice to be out of the wind. *The sun appeared sporadically from behind the clouds, and we lingered over the campfire, even taking time to heat water for bathing and wash-ing underwear. It felt good to take off our clothes and bathe in warmth.* A short hike over the ridge revealed an American tree sparrow, perched atop a 2-m spruce in a dwarf willow thicket. The bird seemed pleased to be tossed back-and-forth by the wind. I couldn't share its enthusiasm.

At three in the afternoon we put on the water, as the wind dropped to a steady breeze, and the rollers on the large bay no longer broke off-shore. It looked canoeable. We made slow but steady progress along the bay.

"This isn't so bad, but don't tell the wind. We don't want to make it mad."

Ninety minutes later we turned into a 12-km arm extending directly north. The wind lay in ambush, and immediately sent breaking waves rolling into our path. *We were making so little progress that we agreed to stop.* At 5:00 pm we stood on the shore.

We trudged up a small ridge above a bog, again thinking we'd never reach Baker Lake.

"We can't possibly paddle 12 km directly into this wind."

We lay down in a small depression in the tundra, and were greeted with the pleasingly sweet essence of crushed northern Labrador tea. We also experienced why tundra plants so commonly grow no more than 20 cm high. At their height, we were out of the wind, baking in sunshine and enjoying silence.

After about 20 minutes, we convinced ourselves that the wind was slackening, so we resumed paddling. We made reasonable progress until we rounded a point extending into the lake. Waves crashed over the bow, and we turned to run before them. Driving hard for shore, and leaping out to avoid broaching, we again stood on shore. *We were very depressed to have put so much effort into paddling against the wind, only to make almost no headway.*

Once more we trudged back up the ridge, lunch in hand. Chinese noodles steeped in the thermos of water heated at breakfast. Crackers and cheese followed the soup. Kathleen has done an excellent job with the meals, which are certainly highlights of the trip.

As the cheese disappeared, we looked at each other with hopeful disbelief.

"Is the wind really stopping?"

"I think it is!" replied Kathleen.

Back in the boat for two full hours of paddling into a gentle breeze. Gliding into twilight, periodically circled by a flock of curious oldsquaws, we finally were able to develop a paddling rhythm.

The wind returned as we neared the first of the marked rapids leading to the Thelon Canyon. We exchanged our light, wooden flat-water paddles for the heavier, more rigid, river paddles, which are far superior at moving and side-slipping the boat in white water.

The first two rapids were only riffles—almost disappointing. The next five rapids occurred in close sequence on a bend to the right. We eddied out on the inside corner to assess the upper stretch of foam. A ledge followed by a few rocks, with sufficient room to make the necessary moves left, right, and left. We ran it. Then a series of rocks in shallow water, which required only that the canoe be kept parallel with the current. We ran it. Our spirits were high. One rapid to go.

We eddied out on river-right to scout. A serious ledge, with a 2-m souse hole, extending all the way across the river. Through binoculars, we could see a possible sneak route on the distant left bank.

"Can we ferry all the way across without going over the ledge?"

"I think so," agreed Kathleen.

Back in the boat for a must-make ferry. Broad-siding a rock or losing the ferry angle would likely be fatal. The water was not pushy, and we held our position for the 200 m across to the left shore.

Walking to the ledge revealed about 2 m of runnable water between the shoreline and the vicious souse hole below the ledge.

"It's getting late in the day, and we're tired. Why don't we line it?" Kathleen suggested.

Usually, if you can't run a rapid, you can't line it either. We would have infinitely more control of the boat, in the boat, with paddles in hand. Attempting to guide a boat through rapids only with bow and stern lines held from the shore often results in the canoe turning broadside and broaching on rocks. This rapid was probably runnable, though, with a reasonably clear channel next to shore. We just didn't wish to risk a mistake so close to the souse hole, from which canoe and paddlers might never reappear.

Thirty minutes later, we drifted downstream, in complete calm and perfectly clear skies. Floating into a pink northern horizon, we are happy with today's achievements. *We are now camped at 12:30 am, perched above the Thelon River, about 7 km above the dreaded Thelon Canyon portage. We ran seven of the rapids marked in this section, and are encouraged that maybe we can run some of the Thelon Canyon. Michael lined one rapid tonight—a ledge that extended almost completely across the river. We are not accustomed to ledges; so far we don't like them. Ledges afford so few canoeing options.*

For me, it takes only a few days of living—in the open—on the land, before I become enveloped by a sense of quiet exhilaration. It is as though the very power of the earth and the wind penetrate to my soul, and I truly never feel so free, so strong, and so alive, as when I am paddling down a wilderness river. If the wind can be unceasing, so can we. If the rapids provide challenges, we can meet them.

Lying in the tent, we hear the muffled thunder of the Thelon Canyon waiting for our descent tomorrow. This tundra landscape seems limitless and supremely powerful. Nonetheless, we feel at home in this landscape, and share its power and limitless possibilities. We are confident that we shall persevere.

Preparing to portage in Upper Thelon.

Saturday, July 10

An un-runnable 5-km canyon is a blunt leveler of confident men. We made nine km today; four by water, five by portage. At three loads each, we traversed 25 km by land. We brought up the packs in stages, leap-frogging each pile spread along the canyon rim. We began portaging at 2:00 pm, and finished at 1:00 am. A 5-km un-runnable canyon swiftly imposes humility on those who believe they have acquired the power of vast space and lurking winds.

Heads bent down beneath heavy packs, we noted two new plants: an Arctic arnica and a yellow lousewort. Heads up, returning to the trailing pile of gear, we saw a Harris' sparrow and a rough-legged hawk. Soaring and circling above the canyon walls, the hawk's thin whistle admonished us for trespassing into its rodent-hunting preserve.

Beneath the packs again, heads humbly bowed to earth, we saw reminders of portaging colleagues of previous years.

Campfires of those who failed, or chose not to complete their task in a single day. A broken tent peg—a fallen and forgotten aluminum plate—all silent but certain emblems of the true misery of the portage trail.

In the tent at 2:00 am; granola, gorp and sausage for dinner. Much too tired to prepare a hot meal. A 5-km, unrunnable canyon is a formidable challenge, and I'm relieved to be at the end of this portage trail.

Sunday, July 11

Considering our difficult day yesterday, which extended late into the evening, we rose surprisingly early—10:00 am. I think anxiety and tension triggered our internal alarms. We had ended our portage 0.5 km before the Clarke River, but access to the Thelon remained difficult. We would need to lower the canoe and packs 15 m down a nearly vertical cliff of eroding, fractured sandstone. I fell asleep last night already thinking that the Clarke would offer easier access to moving water.

A short saunter to the Clarke over mostly open terrain proved easy. Although nearly as steep, the cliff face above the Clarke River was mostly covered with dwarf birch and alder, which offered much more stable footing. Neither of us relished extending our portage by 0.5 km, but the very difficult access to the Thelon Canyon below our camp drove us back into harness.

We first moved our gear about a third of the distance, to a sunny area in the shelter of a thin strip of white spruce, where we prepared a thoroughly leisurely breakfast in the morning warmth. Smothered in butter and jelly, our bannock was the most enjoyable of the trip.

By 4:00 pm, we were moving down the Clarke River, and rejoined the Thelon above a large island with steep cliff faces all around. Picking our way through the shallow riffles and rocks between the island and the left bank, our spirits soared as we faced only one more rapid, purported in the NWT guide as being runnable. No qualifications. Runnable. As we neared the rapid, an ominous ledge, with 2-m souse holes, stretched between both banks. No route was obvious or apparent. We beached our canoe on river-left to scout.

Very dejectedly, we forced our way along the ridge, through spruce swamp and willow bogs. Kathleen offered her pouting perspective of the prospect before us.

"I don't want to portage anymore."

The inside bend on river-right was too risky. A run down the centre was unthinkable. On river-left, however, a 1-m strip of water between the shore and the ledge beckoned. Access to the strip was guarded by two successive diagonal waves deflecting into the ledge and companion souse hole. The water wasn't too pushy, though, and the remainder of the run along the canyon wall could be completed in relatively calm water.

Back in the canoe, floating toward the thundering ledge, my mouth, as usual, expressed my worry by drying instantly. We easily crossed the first, small diagonal wave. The second curling crest of water proved larger than anticipated. Slicing across with forward strokes, the bow entered the eddy as the stern dipped precariously into the souse hole. Powering forward, and rocking only slightly, we safely turned up into the narrow eddy.

We had done it! We had avoided the portage. Turning tightly, we rode the eddy line along the canyon, making sure to avoid the water heading left into the undercut cliff.

Ten minutes later, we enjoyed our gorp break at the Hanbury River confluence, before being driven back to the water by the most numerous mosquitoes experienced so far.

At 8:30 pm we were in camp, squatting before our fire, sipping brandy and immensely enjoying a shepherd's pie. Neither of us could remember the last time we had experienced a slow-paced, relaxing dinner.

We had travelled only 12 km today, and are about 60 km behind schedule. The arduous upper Thelon is behind us, and virtually no obstacle remains before us for the next couple of weeks. I'm sleepy and tired, but very relaxed.

After many days of wind, storm and anxiety, tonight is calm and peaceful. We are camped just downstream of the Hanbury junction. Yesterday we encountered the Thelon Canyon, where we had expected a portage of perhaps 3 km. Instead, we portaged more than 5 km over difficult terrain, including bogs, willow thickets, spruce stands, huge boulders, and tundra. Scouting the portage, dragging along our hand-held buckets, required about 4 hours for the round trip. We then had two more loads each to carry along the canyon ridge. We completed this transport of gear by leap-frogging one pack ahead, and then returning for the second. Each leg of the portage became progressively more difficult. Eventually, I wasn't even able to stand up beneath the 30-kg loads, unless Michael lifted the packs while I struggled to gain my feet. After 11 hours, I was completely exhausted, and very relieved, when I dropped the last pack at the end of the portage trail.

Well, almost the end of the portage trail. During our scouting along the canyon, we selected a stopping point where we could reach the river only by climbing down a steep, unstable cliff. We camped last night at the top of this cliff, knowing that we faced a very difficult challenge to lower the canoe to the water. This morning we found an easier way to the water's edge about 0.5 km further downstream. So, after breakfast, we finished the portage, loaded the canoe, and set off in quickly-flowing water.

Just before the Thelon joins the Hanbury River, the map indicates a rapid described by the NWT guide as runnable. When we first approached the rapid, we could see only a continuous line of waves curling across the entire river. A good trail led up the cliff, on river-left. Does this path indicate a portage trail? After yesterday's exhausting portage, we weren't prepared to hike up the cliff, push through the willow thickets and spruce, and scramble down the other side. We were very discouraged. Scouting from the trail, we identi-

fied a sneak-route on river-left, just wide enough for our canoe to pass in relatively calm water. After skirting by the ledge, we would then need to power to river-left to avoid the curling waves below the drop. We appreciated our river skills and confidence, which allowed us to avoid another day of portaging. Our leans came in particularly handy, as the curling wave momentarily caught and held our stern in the souse hole below the ledge.

We had finally reached the Hanbury River, our quest for these last two weeks. We had hoped to rest on its banks, to celebrate our accomplishment of completing successfully the first third of our Thelon River trip. The afternoon was windy and rainy, and the bugs were the worst we have experienced so far. We continued downstream to our camping spot of tonight.

We celebrated the end of our second week with a relaxing dinner and a glass of brandy. I am entertained by a semi-palmated plover that repeatedly scurries by to "peep" at me. She doesn't seem concerned—just curious and friendly. One of the nicest parts of this trip is living naturally with all the birds and geese. Quite often, birds perch within eye-sight—so close that binoculars become unnecessary.

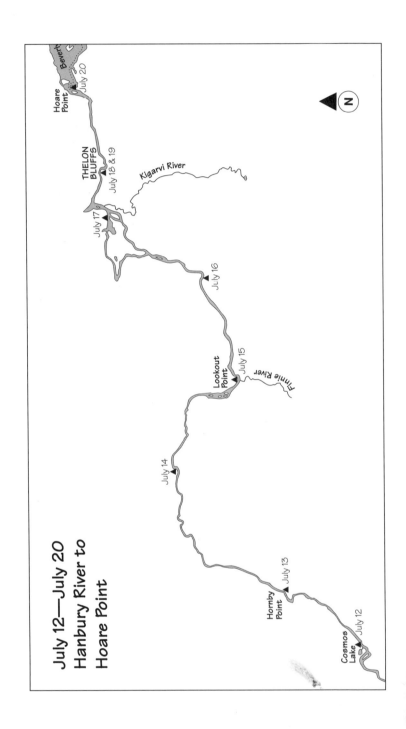

July 12—July 20
Hanbury River to
Hoare Point

N

Hoare Point
Beverl
July 20

THELON BLUFFS
July 18 & 19

Kigarvi River

July 17

July 16

Lookout Point
July 15

Finnie River

July 14

July 13

Hornby Point

Cosmos Lake
July 12

BUGS, BEARS AND HEAT

Monday, July 12

We experienced our first easy day today, which we deserved after two weeks of difficult travelling. We slept until 9:00 am, still needing rest after the canyon portage. In the warm, 19-degree sun we enjoyed a leisurely breakfast for the second successive morning, and then sponge-bathed and washed our hair. The warm water washing away the grime and toil of the previous three days felt exceptionally good. To complete our self-indulgence, we even brushed our teeth.

Just before noon, we began drifting into the sunshine, and within an hour reached Warden's Grove, where Hoare and his assistant Knox built a cabin in 1928. The site served as headquarters for Hoare's assignment as first warden of the newly-created Thelon Game Sanctuary.

An additional over-wintering cabin was constructed in 1977 by six men who spent 18 months journeying from the

MacMillan River in the Yukon, overland to the Nahanni, down the Liard, up the Mackenzie, across Great Slave Lake, and then down the Hanbury-Thelon to Baker Lake and the Hudson Bay coast. Their modern-day epic is superbly chronicled in Chris Norment's book *In The North of Our Lives*.

We continued drifting, enjoying the freedom of unlimited movement and vistas. I'm sure my pleasure in wilderness canoeing relates primarily to this freedom. I believe firmly that the human psyche revels in movement. What else can better explain our species' inherent, nearly constant desire to travel, when staying home would be so much easier and more relaxing? The nomadic peoples probably experience(d) more true freedom than those of us in large houses with larger mortgages that require daily commitment to employment-servitude.

R.M. Patterson, who spent two summers and one winter on the Nahanni in 1927-1928, summarized this freedom best:

> "Those of us who had the good fortune to be on the South Nahanni during those last days of the old north, may in times of hunger or hardship have cursed the day we ever heard the name of that fabled river. Yet, a treasure was ours in the end. Memories of a carefree time, and an utter and absolute freedom which the years can not dim or the present age provide."

I don't dare claim to be in the same league of adventuring and exploring as Patterson, or Norment, or Hoare. Yet, Kathleen and I are adventuring. We paddle through a land inhabited by no other humans. We drift. We camp where we want. We get up and retire when we want. We are the sole arbiters of what we do every hour, minute, and second of every day. We are in paradise.

Paradise must also afford danger to preclude dullness and complacency. Near Grassy Island we saw two Barren-Ground grizzly bears, ambling slowly along the sandy shore. The animals we have encountered on the Thelon invariably become aware of our approaching canoe from what seems like a very great distance. The molting, flightless geese run and flap across the water, sending forth a cacophony of raucous cackling, as they eventually leave the water and literally "head for the hills." The dozen muskoxen at the Mary Francis River stopped grazing, looked up, twitched, moved over the crest of a hill, looked back, twitched, stood still, and stared.

The two grizzlies, without interrupting their lumbering, purposeful gait, simply altered their direction ever so slightly. Angling away from the beach, they disappeared into the dunes and willows. The grizzlies moved because of our unfamiliar human presence; but they didn't look at us, and they didn't flinch. They ignored us with that sarcastic indifference that inevitably develops with the knowledge that you are the most powerful animal in the region. Although we haven't expressed it aloud, I'm sure Kathleen and I will both remember the vision of those two grizzlies as we close our eyes to sleep. True paradise must provide a sharp edge to life.

We paddled leisurely today, enjoying a current with no wind. After the constant struggles in the upper Thelon, this benevolent section of river seemed more like a secure, well-travelled highway. Becoming tourists, we stopped at a riverside attraction—Warden's Grove. Leaving our bug jackets and insect repellent in the canoe, we hiked up hill, over the soggy tundra. The hordes of annoying mosquitoes rising from the bogs surprised us. Weren't we now in a benign land?

Our entourage of mosquitoes followed us into the boat as we left Warden's Grove, and headed down stream. While paddling conditions have improved, two grizzly bears and a moose near Grassy Island remind us we are still in the wilderness.

We are fortunate to be camped on a sandy beach; such beaches are rare and usually small in this section of the river. Inspecting the ground of our potential campsite for signs of recent bear activity, we noticed a circle in the sand—just like the mark left by our white buckets used for storing fresh or aromatic foods. Other people must have been here recently!

Were they tourists? Were they native people who still occasionally hunt caribou and muskoxen in the region? I was distressed to contemplate that we might soon encounter other people in our section of the Thelon River.

Yet, we found no footprints, only other circles of sizes varying between 4 and 30 cm in diameter. We were puzzled. What, in nature, could create these flawlessly round designs? More careful inspection revealed a blade of grass in the centre of each circle. Strong wind rotated the blade, inscribing a perfect circle in the sand! The patterns of designs were quite remarkable in their elegant simplicity.

We had developed a habit of rushing through dinner during our previous long, tiring days. With Michael's encouragement, I'm taking more time to enjoy the food and the campsite during this evening's meal. With time and abundant fuel for heating water, we washed some clothing after dinner. Although our white buckets make great washing machines, they lack a spin-cycle. Wringing the water from long underwear certainly helps to develop new muscles. Michael was able to string a clothes-line between a few trees behind our camp, a rare treat on the tundra.

Tuesday, July 13

The Thelon River below the Hanbury and above Beverly Lake was reportedly only occasionally visited by native peoples. For the Dene, a forest people, too much open tundra existed between tree line and the narrow river corridor of spruce lining both banks. For the Caribou Inuit, a tundra people, the spruce-willow country was too boggy and buggy compared to the shores of Beverly, Aberdeen and Schultz Lakes. We can confirm the Inuit perception. This area harbours substantially more mosquitoes than the upper Thelon. Insects swarm over us, even in the middle of the river. On the upper Thelon, the only mosquitoes to badger us on the open water were those that "hitched" a ride on our canoe or hats.

I was quite relieved yesterday when Kathleen discovered that the sand circles had been fashioned by a single blade or stem of grass, rotating with the wind, rather than by people with their white buckets. Fifteen days have now passed since we last saw another human being. How long could this heady isolation last? All the way to Baker Lake?

Approaching a rocky, exposed point today, where we could lunch with minimum bug assaults, four multi-coloured objects moved strangely on the beach. People! On our beach!

We surely must be on the Trans Canada Highway! Scanning the river bank for the outlet, I noticed bright colors moving on shore. Other people? Suddenly an unfamiliar dilemma confronted us. Should we join them for lunch? Should we stop only to say "hi?" Or, should we ignore them and paddle by?

Politeness seemed to demand that we stop. From them, courtesy required an invitation to share their beach. Although we exchanged trip plans, I think the encounter disappointed both groups; however, Michael did enjoy regaling the audience with his giant fish story. The two men were impressed and pleased; without hesitation, they cast their lines into the water. We had heard a float plane land at the Hanbury/Thelon junction two days ago, and here were its occupants. These two European couples, German and Swiss, paddling inflatable canoes, would travel for two weeks before being picked up at Beverly Lake.

We chatted, relating our stories of the terrible canyon portage, the incessant head winds and the lack of current. After lunch, all 6 of us drifted downstream together. *The afternoon passed quickly as we floated by trees rubbed clean of bark by muskoxen. Three times we stopped to observe these animals for which the sanctuary was established. A pair of tundra swans entertained us as we trailed them down the river. We were not nearly so entertained by our mosquito passengers, who took unfair advantage while we were preoccupied with paddling.*

We landed at Hornby Point, and commiserated in our disappointment at not being able to find the graves of three men who starved here in 1926-27, and who are now forever remembered for their heroic, but needless deaths. *Edgar Christian's diary, found in the cabin stove, details their last days of suffering. Having read the diary, we felt obliged to visit their graves. The area is now overgrown, and though we searched for two hours, we did not find the cabin or graves.*

Leaving Hornby Point, Kathleen and I headed straight across the river to camp on a sandbar, while our fellow voyageurs from Europe paddled slightly upstream to establish their camp on the ridge. Our tents are visible to each other, approximately 400 m apart. Our meeting with these four interlopers on our river has been amiable and not intrusive. But interlopers they are, as we surely are to them. We shall not likely visit each other again.

Our tent is pitched on a sand flood plain between two rivulets. Although it rained for about 5 minutes as we began to eat, we enjoyed a pleasant chili and corn bread dinner.

As soon as dinner ended, Kathleen and I retreated quickly to the tent to avoid the clouds of bugs. I always enjoy watching their frustration trying to get at us through the netting. I also savour the retribution when the few that manage to accompany us into the tent are now at our mercy; unfortunately for the mosquitoes, mercy is a commodity not extended to our flying, buzzing tent mates.

For the last few evenings, it has been usual for wasps to circle and buzz around our tent, obvious insect anomalies among the hordes of mosquitoes. I assumed the wasps were attracted to the colour and landing platform of the nylon shelter. As this evening's wasp hovered back and forth across the netting, it suddenly landed on a mosquito and flew away with its prey! The flying insect predator repeated this process several times, which brought additional joy to my evening. Our tent provided a mosquito-free haven for us, and doubled as a synthetic/biological trap for mosquitoes. A nice way to end the day.

Wednesday, July 14

Yesterday evening, Kathleen and I were 65 km and two days behind schedule. We had appreciated two leisurely paddling days, and planned to be on the river by 9:00 am. We hoped to travel 65 km, thereby completing two days of our itinerary in a single day.

Kathleen didn't bring her watch. I brought mine primarily to be sure of the day. We haven't yet set the alarm, allowing our bodies to receive the rest they require. I didn't wake until the sun warmed my face at 7:00 am.

During breakfast, a storm began to develop in the south, coming towards us on a fairly brisk wind. We hurried our packing, and were gliding downstream just before 10:00 am.

Racing before the storm, propelled by a strong current and assisted by a tail wind, we covered 20 km in just over two hours; however, the storm inevitably caught us, and we paddled until 1:00 pm in a grey drizzle. The poor weather actually aided our goal of covering distance, as we thought only of paddling, and not of lounging on shore. We stopped at 6:45 pm. Nine hours of paddling. Sixty km travelled. Only 40 km behind schedule.

I'm disappointed to spend so much time worrying about our schedule, but we really must be in Baker Lake by August 7. We must be in Vancouver by August 16 to resume our commitments to employment and mortgage. Even here, on the Barren Grounds, professional and personal obligations inject themselves obtrusively.

At lunch we took time to photograph lupines with raindrop-jewels held in their palmate leaves. We also photographed mountain avens, the floral emblem of the Northwest Territories, growing in a pleasing mosaic with large-flowered wintergreens.

We have experienced an extraordinary wildlife day on the river: several bands of muskoxen; innumerable Canada geese (some now able to fly); Bonaparte's gulls swooping and diving in loose flocks with Arctic terns; a fox unsuccessfully but madly chasing a lone goose along the shore; our second wolf, patrolling for nesting birds along the river's edge. Like the first wolf, this silent, patient predator seemed surprised by our presence. It looked briefly directly at us, as if filing information, and then stepped aside into the dense willows.

We're in the tent at 9:00 pm, studying our topographic maps and identifying plants collected near camp: northern sweet vetch and beach pea. Growing together, these magenta and blue-and-white flowers complement each other so very well. The land rests quietly. The rain falls gently. The wind wafts calmly. Outside our tent, the mosquitoes buzz harmlessly. It's been a very good day.

Abundant wildlife and easy paddling attracts canoeists to this section of the river. Our day was filled with wildlife. I have been especially intrigued by Canada geese. In Vancouver parks, geese are so common that I don't pay much attention to their urban life-styles. Here on the Thelon River, I've appreciated the opportunity to experience their more natural behaviours and adaptations. When flightless during molting season, geese instantly flee from danger, whether on land or water. Following what we thought was an otter in the river, we were surprised to discover a goose, swimming with only the top of its head above the water. On land, entire flocks of geese head straight up steep banks on foot, a sight that always astonishes me.

We have chased thousands of geese ahead of us down the river. Michael worries that we may be unintentionally herding all these geese to Baker Lake. We are not a goose's only worry. Today we saw a fox chasing a goose, which eventually escaped safely to the river.

The weather remained cool and cloudy throughout the day, with only a little rain. Good paddling weather. We passed the afternoon enveloped in the aromatic fragrance of northern sweet vetch. On one wide, straight, river section, we observed 20-30 acrobatic gulls and terns diving for bugs. As the strong current sped us down the river, we counted 17 muskoxen, and watched an Arctic wolf along the river's edge. *We are still a day behind schedule, but intend to catch up tomorrow, which had been originally planned as a layover day.*

Thursday, July 15

Again we slept late, until 8:00 am. Even then, I forced myself up reluctantly. Because we wanted to be on the river as soon as possible, we prepared a quick breakfast of oatmeal on the back-packing stove.

On the river at 10:20, beneath a warm sun, we floated before a strong current. We stopped for lunch on a cobblestone island, where we basked in 29-degree temperatures. We shared our lunch spot with a placid, munching muskox, the 4th we had seen during the morning.

The wind remained completely still. We ate lunch in an eerie calm; not a movement or sound around us. We almost welcomed the mosquitoes that assaulted us in the afternoon, as their attacks seemed to prove that we existed in this surreal world.

After lunch, the river turned south, toward a darkening sky pressing swiftly toward us on a south wind. By two o'clock we were paddling in rain, thunder and lightning, mixed with periods of bright, warm sun, as the fronts passed behind us to the north.

Thunder clouds built in the vast sky during the afternoon. Our paddling entertainment focussed on predicting if and when a storm would overtake us. Dampened as we passed through the edge of a thunder storm, we stopped for a snack break.

We lightly struck shore, and Kathleen hopped out to pull the canoe out of the current. I glanced to the left, as I noticed movement out of the corner of my eye. Then, as calmly and as casually as I could, I said "Yikes, Kathleen! Get back in the boat!"

Michael seemed to be slow following me onto the beach. What was he saying?

M. Pitt

Standing on an exposed ridge to escape 18 quadzillion bugs.

M. Pitt

Our bug-free kitchen at the Mary Francis River.

"Get - back - into - the - canoe."

Without looking, I knew it must be a bear! Quickly back into the boat, I was eager to back-paddle away from the advancing Barren-Ground grizzly, now only 15 m away. Michael, however, admonished me to

"Hold still while I get my camera."

During the minute or two we sat against the shore for Michael to take the picture, the bear continued to saunter towards us. As we slowly backed into the river, the bear continued down to the water's edge, stopping only after putting both massive front paws in the river. He stared at us, looked around, and then ambled back into the willows.

The bear wasn't aggressive. Just curious about what had disturbed his nap. I snapped a photograph—the bear's brown image filling the frame. I hoped I would never get a better picture opportunity of a grizzly. We quickly canoed away, happy to relinquish our gorp position to the bear on the beach.

Searching for a campsite that afternoon, I discounted everything on river-left, the bank where the bear lived! Having found no suitable camp, we eventually reached Lookout Point just after 5:00 pm, again beneath clear skies heated to 24 degrees by the afternoon sun.

The delta of the Finnie River, opposite Lookout Point, made the right bank too boggy for camping. Discouraged, we nevertheless decided to hike up the steep bank to scan our surroundings. The flat, dry point, with a wonderful, unimpeded view in all directions, convinced us to portage our gear up the 20 m embankment to make camp on the plateau. We looked forward to a relaxing evening with our spaghetti dinner, chatting and viewing the Barrens stretching before us.

By the time we had set up camp, the storms had passed and we enjoyed relaxing in the warm sun before dinner. While observing storms developing in the distance, we ate quickly, washed, and stowed our gear for the evening. Prepared to retreat hastily into the tent if necessary, we enjoyed our perfect view of storms approaching from the distant southern horizon.

Just after 8:00 pm, the sky darkened, indicating the approach of another brief shower. We put on our paddling jackets to watch the storm. *Suddenly, the sky opened to drench us.* High winds hurled torrential rains in 50-km/hour gusts, as thunder and lightning overwhelmed our exposed position. Too late and too wet to flee to the tent, we decided to wait out the storm. Forty minutes later, we still stood with our backs to the wind and rain. Our foolish bodies poured with water, while our new, $300.00 rain suits lay dry in our packs. *At storm's end, we literally poured water out of our boots!* We hurriedly retrieved dry clothes from the packs, stripped off our soaking clothes, stored them beneath the vestibule, and ran with wild gyrations into the tent ahead of the swarming, frenzied mosquitoes. Apparently it's impossible to have an uneventful day while adventuring on the Thelon River.

As I lay in the tent, drying out and warming up, I mentally reviewed our day. For the first time, I realized that we were finally back on schedule! This reassuring fact had temporarily been lost in all the excitement of the bear and the storms.

Friday, July 16

A day where the seemingly impossible may actually occur; nothing eventful has befallen us so far. The day began much like yesterday. Up at 7:00 am in 10-degree weather. The sun soon burned away the heavy mist, revealing our splendid view, as we spread our wet clothes on the ground to dry. Lighting the fire proved difficult and frustrating because of wet wood, but eventually we cooked our morning bannock, and embarked down river at 10:40 in 24-degree heat.

Lunch on a cobblestone beach—26 degrees—with the inevitable thunderclouds appearing on the southern horizon. At mid-afternoon we still paddled in ideal conditions; calm, warm, and sunny. We stopped to photograph a group of 14 muskoxen.

Leaving the shore, a male Canada goose sounded his alarm note incessantly as we drifted downstream together. As we passed his family on the shore, the goose dove, like a loon, reappearing in the sneak position after staying under approximately 30 seconds.

Ten minutes later we stopped to put on rain gear, as the storm overtook us. By 4:30 pm, we arrived at camp, waited for the storm to pass, then cooked and dined in sunlight and warmth.

We're in the tent early tonight, prepared for the thunder and rain that now sweep toward our ridge above the river. We are on schedule, and will likely gain a day by reaching the Thelon Bluffs, 60 km distant, in two rather than three days. We're looking forward to our rest day there, our first since July 4. We hope we can pass through the Bluffs without having to portage.

Our camp is very pleasant this evening, on a ridge with a view, surrounded by lupines, alpine arnica, aromatic wormwood, star-flowered chickweed, liquorice root and mountain avens. Nothing eventful has happened, and we have thoroughly enjoyed our evening.

We experienced a milestone today on this 19th day of our trip. For the first time, we began and ended our day exactly as proposed on the itinerary. Twice before we have begun the day as originally intended, but had been stopped sooner than planned because of wind. Even though our paddling day was short, we travelled 34 km, and, for the first time, we saw muskoxen with babies!

Good weather persisted through early evening, which allowed us to enjoy a less rushed dinner than the previous couple of days. Weather is interesting on the tundra, not only because it affects all daily activities, but also because so much weather can be seen. We had expected storms this evening, as we noticed dark thunderclouds developing in the south after a day of southerly winds. The wind has now shifted to east-northeast, however, and the storms are literally stalled on the opposite side of the river. I hear a lot of thunder in the distance. Is it coming our way? I hope not.

Saturday, July 17

After escaping last night's thunderstorms, this morning we ate breakfast and packed under partly cloudy skies. Once again we paddled in unreal stillness; not a breath of wind—even the geese fell silent. On shore, without the action of paddle slicing through water and canoe rippling the river surface, I felt almost dizzy. I stomped along the beach, reassured by the sound of my own footsteps.

After another short day on the river, a thunderstorm forced us into the tent before dinner. I prefer to stay in the tent as much as possible, however, when bugs are as bad as they are tonight.

A Loon Air plane flew low over the river today. The pilots told us they'd look for us whenever their flights brought them near our route. It's reassuring having someone watching out for us.

We paddled away from the beach beneath overcast skies. Sixteen degrees at 10:30 in the morning. The river corridor now split low banks of willow between broad expanses of open tundra. Only a few pockets of white spruce remained. Because of the more open terrain, we again saw long-tailed jaegers, for the first time since reaching the Hanbury/Thelon junction. Also because of the changing landscape, we saw no muskoxen today; hopefully, the more open tundra will reveal herds of caribou that follow the river to calve north of Beverly Lake. We've been disappointed to see only two single caribou so far.

This afternoon on the river was truly superb. Just the kind of conditions and moods that compel Kathleen and me to canoe wilderness rivers. The air and land were completely still, as though we were travelling through a painting. Only the ripples of our wake stirred the water's surface. The only sounds were those of our paddles and the distant distress calls of Canada geese.

It was an unforgettable two hours, when Bill Mason's "Song of the Paddle" rolled across the tundra. I am very grateful to have the opportunity to experience the crystal silence of this place. It is also very satisfying to see and to know that the Barrens do indeed lie, still, in grace.

We stopped early (3:30 pm) and pitched camp on a low ridge above a cobblestone beach. We were only 20 km from the Thelon Bluffs, an easy jaunt for tomorrow. The 29-degree heat hung oppressively around us. Why is the tundra so hot? With no shade, day or night, we hoped for a breeze to quickly bring our usual afternoon thunderstorm.

Relief came at 6:00 in the evening. Napping and reading in the tent, we felt a cool wind. Minutes later, thunder, lightning and strong gusts enveloped our tent. I relished the luxury of lying quietly, cool and dry, all the chores done, on schedule, listening to the rain striking the fly.

Sunday, July 18

Another overly-hot day; 24 degrees at 9:30 in the morning. The Barrens continue to be heated by a hazy, south wind, which smells of wood smoke. We speculate that the boreal forests of northern Saskatchewan and Manitoba may be ablaze with wildfires.

The day on the river was unusually quiet, as the geese numbers dwindled substantially. We saw only one moose, at the north end of Ursus Islands, and only one muskox, where the river bends southeast toward the Thelon Bluffs. As with all other muskoxen, this individual was browsing willows on the left bank. Apparently muskoxen are Socialist creatures; we have seen none on the right bank.

For a late lunch, we stopped at a cabin operated by the Water Quality Branch of Environment Canada. I enjoyed the opportunity to sit down at a table, out of the wind and sun, and away from the bugs. The stagnant cabin air felt stuffy and stifling after three weeks in the open. We soon left, drifted lazily downstream, and made camp at the Bluffs.

After the normal afternoon shower and thunder, Kathleen cooked another great dinner, preceded by a glass of brandy to celebrate the halfway point (20 nights) of our journey. Following dinner, two options remained: to walk along the ridge looking for caribou, or to go to bed. It was already late (7:30 pm), and still hot (24 degrees). Bed carried the election by two votes. Besides, we had pitched our tent about 400 m from the river, on a knoll affording commanding views out the front and back doors. We could see caribou from a prone position as easily as we could see caribou by struggling up the ridge.

Tomorrow is a rest day, our first in two weeks. Just thinking about not having to get up, pack the gear, and paddle downriver comforts me. It feels good to get an early start on the rest day.

Half the days of the trip are over, and we are one day ahead of schedule. Our itinerary calls for a rest day tomorrow, so we can rest and still have an extra day to put toward the lakes section.

We paddled effortlessly today in the intense heat. So much has changed since the Hanbury junction. We travel in complete calm; at most, a cooling breeze drifts gently towards us from the south. Only a few geese live along this section of the river. We encounter mostly large animals—usually muskoxen—and today a moose.

We are camped at the Thelon Bluffs, comprised of high rolling hills. Rapids located at the bend, just down stream from our camp, are described by various authors as either a necessary portage or runnable. We'll scout tomorrow, but from the end of the first bend, the rapids appear runnable. The Thelon Canyon portage has put me right off portaging. I hope we can run these rapids.

We ate lunch indoors this afternoon, at a government cabin upstream from our camp at the Bluffs. The novelty of tables and chairs and NO bugs only partly compensated for the stuffy, dark, confining feeling of the Water Service Recording station. A log book containing the adventures and misadventures of Water Service staff and river travellers made entertaining lunch reading. Only one account had been entered for this year, by a party who passed here

5 days ago. While Michael added our story, I found a mirror. Not having seen myself in 4 weeks, I expected to see a healthy, tanned face. I look more like a lobster!

Monday, July 19

We spent the second layover day of the trip leisurely washing people and clothes. The brisk wind keeps the mosquitoes down, and quickly dries our laundry. I reorganized and checked food supplies. We are well-provisioned in all areas. The only spoilage is some mould on the outside of the cheese. At the bottom of a white bucket, I discovered the orange that I had stuffed there as we taxied down the lake for our flight to Lynx Lake. The fresh fruit was a real treat after three weeks of dried food.

A thick smoke, blown in by the strong, south winds, obscured our view as we hiked to our highest elevation on this trip. We were pleased to confirm that the rapid is easily runnable.

The weather continues to fascinate me as I try to anticipate what will happen next. I resolved to live in the moment on this trip, but I am so tempted to try to predict the weather. Will today be good paddling weather? Will we be drenched by rain?

Because we've been living outdoors, continually exposed to wind and sun, my hands are becoming very dry and cracked. One of my major concerns is keeping my hands healthy, as they are essential for everything we do on the river: cooking, packing, making camp, and—most importantly—paddling. During all these tasks, hands are constantly exposed to potential injury and damage. After nearly three weeks of cooking over a fire, soot fills, blackens and grinds the cracks in my hands. Washing them with hot water and detergent only makes them drier. I now wear protective gloves when washing the dishes; hand cremes don't seem to help. While on the river, I keep my hands covered as much as possible by wearing gloves and sun screen.

Although our rest day was relaxing and rejuvenating, we stayed fairly busy. I arose at 6:30 am, intending to catch a grayling for breakfast. The rocky shoreline produced many snags, two lost lures, one small (15 cm), unknown species of fish, and no grayling.

The wind blew all last night, and continued throughout the day, which was perfect for us. No bugs. After another great bannock breakfast, we stripped, cleaned our entire bodies, and then washed all our dirty clothes. Spread on dwarf birches and flat, lichen-encrusted tundra rocks, the laundry dried very quickly in the never-ending wind.

We then inspected gear for required repairs, and inventoried food and supplies. Using cold-cure, a 2-mixture, glue-anything epoxy, I repaired the bow cane seat, and reattached the soles of my hiking boots, sealed in place with ample amounts of duct tape. A few too-curious mosquitoes are now part of the inner sole and fabric of my footwear. After applying a small patch over a hole in one of the canoe-pack's vinyl liners, we sat down to lunch.

In the afternoon, we hiked to the top of the Bluffs to gain a better view of our world. Camp below looked so very small and insignificant in the grey, low, undulating vastness surrounding our knoll. At our feet, Kathleen spotted small clumps of thrift—pink petals already fading to merge with the brown-grey colours of their dry, wind-blasted ridge.

The shoreline dunes along the Thelon Bluffs are dominated by tall stands of beach rye-grass. For some reason, the geese had overlooked this particular luxuriant pasture. The lush grass seemed out of place here, where all other herbs remain so short-statured. According to Page Burt, in her book *Barrenland Beauties*, the Inuit use the leaves of this grass to weave baskets.

Burt also reports that the Inuit use white Arctic heather as a fuel. Because of its high oil content, this woody species burns easily, even when green. Returning to camp, we collected some as kindling, eager to test this traditional wisdom. I'm pleased to report that the twigs burst into flame, and quickly started our dinner fire.

We've now completed approximately half our journey, and our supplies remain plentiful. We used only 1.3 litres of white gas in the upper Thelon, and only about 0.2 liters since the Hanbury. Slightly more that 10 litres remain for Beverly, Aberdeen, and Schultz Lakes, which likely have less firewood.

We also have plenty of time, having reached the Thelon Bluffs one day early. We are well-rested, and seem to possess sufficient rest days as insurance against high winds. I hope the second half of the journey is as successful as the first half.

Tuesday, July 20

The day began overcast and slightly cooler, only 19 degrees at 9:30 am. While portaging the 400 m from camp back to the river's edge, we tentatively identified a pectoral sandpiper. It had the appropriate breast marking, made the correct sound (assuming I can interpret "prrt" correctly), but didn't zig-zag when flushed. Positive confirmation must wait until we play our bird tapes in Vancouver.

We easily negotiated the rapid by entering the Thelon Bluffs from river-centre, and then running the eddy-line on river-right to avoid the medium-sized haystacks on river-left. We relaxed, believing we had run the last rapid until the outlet of Aberdeen Lake.

Around the bend, however, appeared a series of rapids not marked on the maps or even mentioned in the NWT river profile. These rapids were shallow and rock-strewn, exactly like those on which we learned our white-water skills in southern British Columbia. We simply kept our canoe parallel to the flow of water, and reached the bottom of the rapid unscathed and upright.

At 11:30 am, a soft rain began to fall. Its gentle demeanor provided a soothing, restful quality to the river and Barrens, particularly in contrast to the previous three days of heat. The greyness seemed appropriate to the landscape, and we paddled

contentedly, without speaking except when one of us requested "switch" to rest a paddle-weary side.

After lunch we abruptly turned north down the narrow
chute that culminates this section of the river. The sun reap-
peared as we rounded Hoare Point and gazed east down
Beverly Lake, which lay still, stretching before us to the horizon.

Only 3:00 pm, and we pitched camp in the most beautiful
spot so far. From Hoare Point we have views back up the
Thelon and down Beverly Lake. Plenty of firewood lies in large
heaps on the point, piled there as the Thelon empties into
Beverly Lake.

After dinner of chili and corn bread, we luxuriated in the
sun, backs against a rock, sipping tea, looking through half-
closed eyes down Beverly Lake, lulled to near-napping by the
soft waves breaking on the shore. I'm more comfortable and at
ease here than at any other point of the journey. A near-per-
fect day. If only we had seen caribou. We had seen 18 muskox-
en, including two non-conformists on the right bank; but no
caribou.

*After paddling all day in the rain, we arrived at Hoare Point,
our first camp on the large, tundra lakes. Our itinerary shows 18
days to Baker Lake, including 5 planned for layover or wind. We
are hoping the calm winds of today continue on the lakes.*

*Our quiet dinner preparations were interrupted when three float
planes buzzed low over our heads. Fortunately, they were just saying hello, and quickly flew away, leaving us alone again in this flat
and limitless wilderness. Unfortunately, they left without taking the
mosquitoes with them.*

*Thinking back on these days since we landed at Lynx Lake, I'm
impressed with how quickly we established a daily pattern for our
lives on the river. The familiarity of routine brings comfort and stability to the uncertainty of this adventure. Arising before me,
Michael makes breakfast while I pack the items in the tent and put*

the sleeping bags, therm-a-rests and pillows into their sacks. After cooking breakfast, of which bannock and tea is our favourite, Michael takes the tent down and loads the "sleeping-gear" pack. I pack the pots and cooking utensils, fill the thermos with hot water for lunch, and put the day's dinner into my plastic container to rehydrate. Packs and other items are stowed in their established positions, and the spray deck is stretched and snapped into place.

On reaching camp, I put the tent up, and situate the sleeping gear, books, first aid kit and water bottles, while Michael finds firewood and makes a fire pit. He usually builds me a good kitchen, with flat rocks placed perfectly for convenient pot rests. When I'm ready to begin preparing dinner, Michael starts the fire. Most of the dinners were cooked in Vancouver before they were dried, so they need only to be re-heated. After long, tiring days on the river, we very much appreciate a quick, hot meal. After I cook and wash the dishes, we pack everything not needed during the night. Michael then organizes all the packs under the canoe, and secures the canoe with ropes to rocks and shrubs.

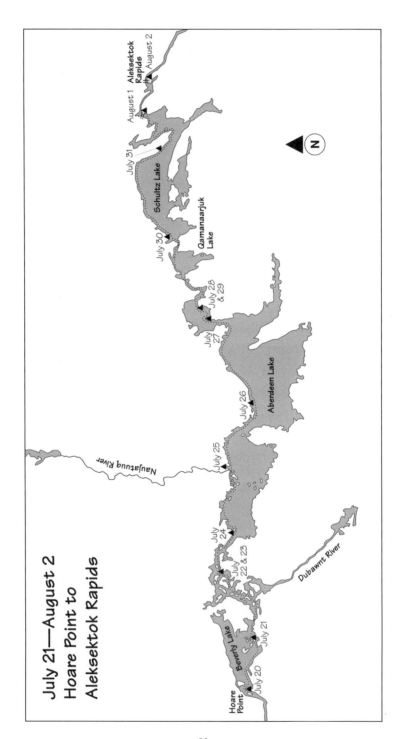

July 21—August 2
Hoare Point to
Aleksektok Rapids

Aleksektok Rapids
August 2
August 1
July 31
Schultz Lake
Qamanaarjuk Lake
July 30
July 28 & 29
July 27
July 26
Aberdeen Lake
July 25
Naujatuuq River
July 24
July 22 & 23
Dubawnt River
July 21
Beverly Lake
July 20
Hoare Point

N

LAKES OF WIND—LAND OF PEACE

Wednesday, July 21

Another quiet day. Very quiet. Virtually no wind, no caribou, no muskoxen and nearly no geese. Except for Lapland longspurs, whose breeding plumage is already fading, we seem to have been left alone on Beverly Lake. The red bearberry flowers have been replaced by firm, green berries, and the mature fruit of the cloudberry now glistens red in moist, tundra depressions.

The weather continues unbearably hot during the Arctic summer. Twenty-six degrees today, with a low last night of 10° C. It must turn awfully cold very soon to reach monthly norms. According to the NWT Thelon River profile, mean daily highs in July equal 16° C, and daily lows average 6° C. All our highs and lows have remained above these averages, and only 10 days remain in July.

We're both really hoping for frost. The bugs, combined with the heat, are beginning to irritate us. It's nearly impossible to sit comfortably outside. We often seek shelter in the tent sooner than we wish after dinner. These bugs will get what's coming to them someday, and I want to be here to enjoy it. Maybe frost will visit us tonight, although this heat makes such an event highly unlikely.

The upper Thelon River seemed more pristine than this section of lake; cans and small piles of garbage too often litter benches overlooking the lake shore. This debris might have been cast aside 30-50 years ago when more people regularly hunted, trapped and travelled on the land. We're ever-vigilant for Inukshuks or tent rings, but so far have seen only what appear to be "modern" creations. This evening, though, on the point opposite Isarurjuag Peninsula, I found two tent rings. They appeared small enough to be realistic, and overgrown enough with northern Labrador tea to be authentic. The rings occupy a prominent position, with views west, north and east. I'm convinced they are truly Inuit tent rings—an exciting thought!

Another beginning. Embarking on the final third of the trip, we paddled leisurely along the south shore of Beverly Lake. In the hot Arctic morning, we rigged a sail. It barely billowed in the slight tail-wind accompanying us; needing one person to direct the sail, we moved more slowly than with both of us paddling. In a strong gust, the canoe scooted across the water; but rounding a point and finding ourselves farther from shore than was comfortable, we abandoned sailing for the more consistent speed and greater stability of two paddlers.

We're camped on a beautiful sandy beach in the warm sun— early afternoon, and good progress achieved. We can relax in comfort for the rest of the day. Unfortunately, the mosquitoes have other plans for us, and we are once again held hostage in our tent.

Working for the Canadian Geological Survey, Joseph Tyrrell convinced his superiors to allow him to explore a possible canoe route through the Barrens from Lake Athabasca to Hudson Bay. His brother James accompanied him, and wrote an account of the 1893

expedition, which I am now reading in Farley Mowat's book
Tundra. *Their route joins ours tomorrow as we pass the confluence*
with the Dubawnt River. We expect the wide watercourse between
Beverly and Aberdeen Lakes, with its many islands, channels and
inlets, to resemble a lake, with no current. James Tyrrell, however,
wrote of this section, "we pulled on with the stream now double its
former strength and flowing again to the northward." Maybe we will
be pleasantly surprised.

Thursday, July 22

Perhaps 100 years ago, "flowing" meant sluggish, still, and mean-
dering. Or perhaps this waterway's character has indeed changed.
We lunched under somber skies, while watching the Dubawnt's
waters mingling with the Thelon's. All afternoon the compass guid-
ed us through the maze of channels. Often, not sure of our location,
we stopped to gain perspective from an island rise.

A new insect made our acquaintance this afternoon. Never bit-
ing, it flies frenetically around, into eyes, nose, ears and mouth.
Even the slightest breeze sends it to the protection of a lee, which
unfortunately the paddler often provides. This afternoon, the bugs
cavorted in our faces, where they were shielded from the slight tail-
wind.

Comparisons to the Tyrrells' trip are unavoidable as we pass
landmarks described in their journal. We may feel frustrated with the
bugs and finding a route, but we know with certainty that we're on
course for Baker Lake. One hundred years before us, the Tyrrells
travelled through an unmapped region, down a river that they only
believed and hoped would take them to Baker Lake. We are already
north of their hoped-for destination, yet the Thelon continues to flow
north. The Tyrrells wondered if this new river might be leading them
to the Arctic Ocean, instead of east to Baker Lake. I can imagine
their relief when, as James describes, "at 64°41'N, it suddenly
swerved around to the east and then to the south-east and bore us
down to the western extremity of a magnificent body of water..."
Our camp is just east of what we now call Tyrrell Passage.

Ever since seeing Chris Norment's book cover, showing three canoes and two people standing on the frozen surface of Schultz Lake in July, I've been concerned about ice on the big lakes. Tomorrow we will enter the largest lake. I'm hoping we don't find ice.

The wind blew gently but steadily all night, and we rose at 6:15 to a morning of overcast skies and 12-degree temperatures. After photographing the tent rings, we hurried through breakfast, packed in a rush, and embarked at 8:45. We established our personal record of only 2.5 hours to prepare ourselves for the canoeing day.

I had previously assumed that it would be impossible to be ready in fewer than three hours; however, we hadn't previously benefited from the motivation provided by swarms of little black flies, approximately 10 mm long. They may not be the infamous biting, black flies of the North, but they're terrible, nonetheless. We shared breakfast with a quadzillion of them. No, actually more like 8 quadzillion. They positioned themselves in clouds about our heads, seemingly for no purpose other than to enter all orifices. Not to bite, simply to antagonize.

Today we would be travelling through a maze of islands, bays and channels created by the deltas of the Thelon, Dubawnt and Tibielik Rivers. I purchased my compass specifically for this section of the trip between Beverly and Aberdeen Lakes. Setting the declination to 6° east, I sighted down the line of travel. The needle pointed exactly to where I expected the narrow east-trending channel to lie! So far, so good.

We set off into a NNE wind, accompanied by several tens of thousands of little buggy passengers. They rode along mostly on our backs and hats, sitting comfortably on the lee side of our bodies. Whenever the wind slackened, even for an instant, or if you turned your head back to check the landscape, the bugs gleefully surged into eyes, nostrils and mouth.

We paddled into the wind silently. I didn't know what Kathleen thought or felt, but I enjoyed the moment. Cool, overcast, low hills; just like the Barren Grounds should be. We entered a narrow channel, presumably taking us to the confluence of the Dubawnt River, but emerged instead into a large bay.

"This can't be right!"

"Do you know where we are?" Kathleen asked, with only a little mistrust in her voice.

"I thought so. We should be coming to the Dubawnt in a few minutes, but this doesn't look right."

Twenty minutes later, and no Dubawnt River. Had we gone into one of the deep, narrow bays by mistake? Were we ascending the Dubawnt itself? In this wind, against a sluggish or non-existent current, we wouldn't know. We stopped to check the compass. We were travelling in exactly the right direction; we couldn't have taken a wrong turn.

"Maybe that channel wasn't the one we were looking for. You did say that the channel looked so narrow on the map that it might not even be passable. This channel seemed wider than that." Kathleen's advice seemed logical.

"Let's keep going, then. The map hasn't been wrong yet."

Ten minutes later we slipped into a very narrow, shallow channel flowing between shore and the low banks of an island. Moments later, we ferried across the sluggish Dubawnt, and beached the canoe for lunch.

J.B. Tyrrell descended the Dubawnt with his brother in 1893. In his journal, J.W. Tyrrell spoke glowingly of the copious amounts of driftwood available once they reached the Thelon. From Tyrrell's journal:

> "That night, camp was pitched on an island and we had a roaring fire of driftwood. We hoped that for some time the supply of fuel might continue, for of late we had been entirely without fire."

Either they celebrated by burning all firewood after their treeless journey down the Dubawnt, or his journal exaggerated reality. We found no firewood, either at the Thelon-Dubawnt junction, or in the 12 km of islands and channels below the confluence.

We did, however, see three caribou, one of which ran wildly back-and-forth, trying vainly to escape the now 12 quadzillion small, black flies. A few kilometres below the confluence, the river offered a special gift—a yellow-billed loon, which breeds only on the Arctic coast, according to our bird book. We never expected to see a yellow-billed loon, either on this trip, or perhaps in our lives. A real highlight of the day!

J.W. Tyrrell spoke of the current carrying them to Aberdeen Lake. We found no current, and continued to stroke hard, hour-after-hour, into the wind.

"Kathleen, I think that land on the left is an island, but I'm not sure. If we're in a bay, we're lost."

"Let me see the map."

We stopped. I explained my understanding of where I thought we were, and Kathleen agreed. We continued paddling. Twenty minutes later we reached a 0.75-km section of open water, crossed in a diagonal, following sea, and rounded the point where we intended to camp. This section of the trip certainly demands confidence with map-reading skills.

No firewood. We decided against camping, and continued paddling into the wind. After leaving what we called "Tyrrell Passage," at 64°41'N, we spotted a few sticks of driftwood on the shore. Like the Tyrrells 100 years before us, we appreciated that the river had now turned east, and it seemed an appropriate place to camp.

A very quick dinner with 16 quadzillion uninvited guests. We fled to our tent-haven at 7:30 pm, with our would-be companions hurtling their buggy bodies against the nylon tent walls. I don't know what these bugs are, but they detract, immeasurably, from the pleasure of our trip.

Friday, July 23

We awoke at 8:00 am, still tired from nearly nine hours of paddling yesterday. During the night, the NNE wind intensified, and now sent 1-m waves across the bay, breaking on the shore in white, running sheets of water. Obviously we wouldn't be going anywhere, at least for a few hours. *We can't paddle, and for one of the first times on this trip, I believe we are responsible for our delay. Last night, with no wind, we could have crossed to camp on the north shore. We knew the north shore was our ultimate goal; we knew the wind generally blows from the north. We also knew the wind comes up unexpectedly. If only we had camped on the north shore, in the lee, we probably could have paddled today.*

Because no immediate need now existed for breakfast, I took time to photograph some lichens and flowers. The diminutive, 1-cm tall ligonberry, was now flowering two weeks after its tundra companions had peaked in their floral displays. A dark lichen grew commonly on the soil surface, frequently forming compact pin-cushion mats similar to moss campion.

I collected some dead crowberry, which makes excellent fire kindling. The dry twigs normally flame quickly, with heat sufficient to ignite the small sticks placed on top. This time, though, the wind instantly extinguished the flames sputtering from my inexpensive lighter and kitchen matches. I then retrieved our special "wind" matches, guaranteed to light and remain burning during windstorms; unfortunately, only the first half of the guarantee proved reliable. Apparently the matches were developed for winds other than those of the Barren Grounds.

Oh well, we still had two backpacking stoves and 10 litres of fuel in reserve. Using a lever-action flint, the stove lighted immediately, and produced a bannock 25 minutes later.

The wind brings at least two benefits, the most important of which is a bug-free environment. The wind also creates a rest day, which we both wanted after yesterday's struggle against headwinds. We sauntered to a knoll one kilometre distant, and stood alone, together, in our world comprised only of wind, water and tundra. No caribou. One Lapland longspur.

Back at camp at noon. The wind continued blowing hard. We retired to the tent to nap and doze. Perhaps the wind will have abated when we wake, and we can still reach Aberdeen Lake today.

Two-thirty. The wind not only persists, but blows even more intensely. We boiled water for soup and tea, and ate a few graham crackers with peanut butter. *Despite enjoying a sunny rest day, I can't help worrying about nearly everything. As the wind increased, so did my concern for the security of our tent pitched on the beach. After our tundra walk and lunch, we moved the tent to the south side of a small rise, where the lessened strain was immediately apparent.* Satisfied with our new location, we crawled in to rest and wait out the storm. *Although it doesn't appear that any progress toward Aberdeen Lake will be possible today, I must remember the pluses of yesterday's decision. Our campsite is much better than would be available on the steep, north shore; and our restful, relaxing tundra walk today represents a trip highlight not likely attainable if we had paddled.*

The wind slackened somewhat around 6:00 pm, and we headed to the cooking area on the beach for another attempt at a wood fire. After a few tries, our beef jerky stew bubbled in the pot. Our success was offset, though, by our 19 quadzillion buggy friends, who had obviously missed us immensely during the wind storm.

When the wind died, about 7:00 pm, we discussed packing and paddling tonight. With four insurance days for the last 15 days to Baker Lake, we shouldn't be in a panic. We'll sleep tonight and hope for calm in the morning; however, I'm apprehensive about this decision.

Although we both felt disappointed to have spent our extra insurance day on shore, we were approximately 8 km ahead of schedule. Pretty good after nearly four weeks since leaving Lynx Lake. Aberdeen Lake could wait for tomorrow. We retired to the tent for tea, our ears caressed by the soft rattling voice of a nearby sandhill crane.

Saturday, July 24

I awoke to the fluttering and banging of the rain fly against the tent walls. "Damn, the wind is up again." Well, at least it's an opportunity to eliminate all that tea without exposing myself to those merciless insects. Even in the middle of the night, in the wind, the air remained warm, about 12 degrees. The night sky, although still light, appeared a bit dusky for the first time on the trip. A deep, crimson colour arched across the northern horizon. These endless days of sunlight are what draw Kathleen and me repeatedly back to the north. We love the freedom to move spontaneously in response to mood, need or whim. Maybe the wind will die by morning. I really don't want to spend another idle day on the beach.

With a sense of foreboding, I awoke to the sound of the tent flapping in the wind. We must get to the north shore. Studying the maps last night, we discovered a safe route to reach this goal, by using a large island just downstream from us for wind protection. Six-thirty am. The wind continues as strong as yesterday. We made tea and bannock, and filled the thermos with hot water for lunch-time soup. *After breakfast, we packed the canoe and sat on shore watching the waves. We must get to the north shore.* Ninethirty. The NNW wind as strong as ever.

"Kathleen, maybe we can canoe along the south shore to that island lying across the channel, and cross over to the north shore on its lee side, where the waves and wind won't be so strong."

"You're right. Maybe we can. We can certainly try. There seem to be fewer whitecaps, let's go."

At 9:45 am we thrust the canoe into the surf. We paddled hard, quartering the canoe into the rollers, away from the waves breaking on shore. We then turned and quartered back toward shore, to avoid taking waves broadside, and to be near land. At 11:00, we had gained about 1 km, and stopped to rest and assess our position.

"That piece of land must not be the island on the map. I don't see any channel around it on the north shore. It just must be part of the bend in the north shore."

"You're right," agreed Kathleen. " What shall we do?"

"Let's cross the open water on the right bank in as narrow a spot as possible, then keep heading down the right shore until we find the island."

"O.K."

Back in the boat, we came to the narrow channel and crossed over easily to continue along the right bank, looking for the island.

"There it is," I said, "but it's awfully low. I thought the map indicated a 20-m contour on the island."

"Maybe the island top coincides with the contour, and it's not really very high."

"Maybe, but it's not sandy like the map suggests."

"You're right, but it's an island," reasoned Kathleen, "and there's only one island. This has got to be it."

"O.K., let's go."

We rounded the island through the narrow passage on river-right, and grounded on shallow rocks. Kathleen hopped out to pull us through, and I noticed that the small current was coming toward us; must be a back-eddy re-entering the main current through this shallow gap.

We headed toward the north bank in the lee of the island. This was working!

We reached the end of the island, and stared across a large body of open water, seething with wind and waves. We had expected a narrow crossing, as indicated on the map. Wrong island. It was too small anyway to have been the right island. It must have been too small to even be represented on the map. We turned back, and continued down the right bank.

"Michael, do you notice that the wind is coming from the southeast now? How can that be?"

"It just must be the effect of funneling through all these islands and channels."

"Yeah, you're probably right." We continued down the south shore in search of the island.

"There it is! Large like it's supposed to be!"

We crossed over. Even with the wind at our backs, we lost ground to the island's shore line. Just as though we were ferrying upstream against a current. Are we going the wrong way!? Where's the sun? Can't see it. Overcast sky everywhere.

"It's one o'clock, Kathleen. Let's stop for lunch. I'd also like to check the compass."

"Good idea. I'd also like to study the map. Things just don't seem right."

On shore, the compass indicated we were heading west instead of east. The wind direction hadn't switched 180 degrees, but still blew from the northwest. The current, albeit sluggish, was indeed coming toward us. None of the topography around us corresponded to our perception of where we were. These facts combined to suggest that we were lost.

Very disheartening. We could spend days trying to locate our position among these islands and channels. *I've never felt so helpless. If we don't know where we've been since leaving camp, how can we ever find our position? Over lunch, we tried to determine our location by matching memories of landmarks passed to likely places on the map.*

"Well, let's suppose we are going west. The compass hasn't been wrong yet. Where would that place us?"

Kathleen looked at the map. "Right here." She pointed to a spot 8 km southwest of our morning camp. "There's that long narrow bay we just passed."

"Yep, you're right. Let's turn around." *As we turned around to paddle north, we were fairly sure of our location; but I wouldn't relax until we reached Aberdeen Lake.*

Back in the canoe. Maps out. Anxiety running high. At 3:30 pm we arrived at a point due east of where we had crossed the narrow channel this morning; unfortunately, we had crossed it going south, sending us back into the maze of islands we had negotiated so successfully two days ago.

"How could we do that? It's obvious we should have come this way."

I think we had been more concerned with avoiding wind and waves, and had lost our concentration on direction. We were both very irritated with the wind, and had been speaking sharply to each other all day, even when agreeing. I had also put my compass away yesterday, declaring that the hard part was over. We had only to follow the left bank all the way to Baker Lake.

So, here we are, at 3:30, exactly where we had been at 11:00 this morning. We hadn't really lost so much time, though. We wouldn't have made this crossing this morning, anyway. The waves had been too high. All we really have lost is the energy expended. Easily replaced, and a very fair price to pay for the experience gained.

We continued up the east side of the large bay, turned west, north and then east around a bluff and came to the island—the same piece of land that we rejected this morning as being part of a bend in the north shore.

We struggled into the wind until 5:30, when we finally reached the lee of the north shore, and stopped for a gorp break. Neither of us wanted to quit without seeing Aberdeen Lake. Back to the canoe. We soon entered a channel with current heading east. At 9:00 pm, we approached Aberdeen Lake. A beautiful sight, not only for its inherent, stoic grandeur, but also for its very tangible affirmation that we had indeed found ourselves.

It's now 12:30 am. It's been a hard day, physically. We paddled 34 km in wind and waves, some of it against the current, and have gained only 16 km. It's also been emotionally difficult dealing with the very real prospect of being lost, with no one available to help us.

It's also been a good day. We found two new plants: seabeach sandwort and mountain sorrel, which tasted very sweet, as promised in Burt's book. We also saw one muskox and four caribou—posing, regally motionless, on ridge tops. Five km before camp we trudged 0.25 km from the river to a stone structure, and stood beside an Inuit caribou ambush.

Most importantly, we dealt successfully with our physical and emotional challenges, and together we reached our goal. All things considered, we will probably remember July 24 as one of life's most memorable days. *Our camp lies about 16 km east of "Tyrrell Passage," just west of Aberdeen Lake. Today's frustrations have given way to the comfort of a snug sleeping bag, and the security of knowing where we are.*

Sunday, July 25

We awoke at 8:00 am to a moderate NNW wind. A perfect wind—not so strong to prevent us from paddling, but strong enough to send the bugs to the shelter of rocks and plants. We lingered over breakfast, but still put on the water by 11:00.

Forty minutes later we rounded a spit, beached the canoe, and walked to the height of land where the Tyrrell party also had stood to gaze with unimpeded vision east down the full expanse of Aberdeen Lake. No land to the horizon. A vista dominated solely by Aberdeen Lake. Kathleen read from Tyrrell's journal:

M. Pitt

Waiting for the wind to subside at "Tyrrell Passage."

K. Pitt

An Inuit caribou blind?

> "It was a lovely, calm evening, when the track of our canoes first rippled the waters of this lake, and as we landed on a bluff point on the north shore, and from it gazed to the eastward over the solitary but beautiful scene, a feeling of awe crept over us."

One kilometre later we stopped at a cabin, where garbage and debris littered the site. Much of this lake stretch appears marred by human debris, particularly empty fuel drums, their red and yellow colours visible from many kilometres away. The NWT government should enact or enforce legislation that requires fuel drums to be retrieved, rather than littering this still largely pristine landscape. Despite the comparative squalor of the cabin, two sandhill cranes rattled happily on their breeding grounds.

We lunched at a magnificently beautiful spot. A long, wide, white, fine-sand beach, in the lee of a 20-m ridge. Warm sun, no bugs. We lounged for an hour, one of the most comfortable interludes experienced thus far. I hated to return to the boat.

The wind continued throughout the day, just strong enough to make us work hard. As we followed the shore line, the wind slightly, but unmistakably changed directions to be always in our face, the better to thwart our aspirations of reaching the Naujatuug River.

The strain of the previous day, followed by only a few hours sleep, took its effect by late afternoon. My strokes became perfunctory, with little strength behind them. In the stern, my inaction remained invisible to Kathleen in the bow. By 7:00 pm, Kathleen had paddled to the Naujatuug River. As a passenger in the stern, I necessarily arrived a few moments later. We fired up the stoves, as no wood was available, ate our spaghetti dinner quickly, and crawled into the tent for our Sunday ounce of brandy. I'm quite tired, and expect to sleep very well.

Leaving camp this morning under overcast skies, the freedom afforded by endless vistas was supplanted by a mood of constraint. Like a blanket flung over a bed, the somber, grey, cloud-covering seemed about to envelop and smother us. The north-western horizon, where the straight edge of the cloud blanket still revealed brightness, afforded our only hope. As we paddled along the lake, the covering was slowly pulled south-east, returning to us that mystical feeling of unlimited potential for movement.

Completing our journey on schedule is not guaranteed. Despite a head-wind today, we gained 32 km; but tomorrow we could be grounded. A late arrival in Baker Lake will cause worry, especially for my parents. While planning this trip, I perceived that only injury or some other horrific event could prevent our arrival as scheduled; consequently, if we were late, I wished for a search-and-rescue to begin as soon as possible. Recognizing now that we could be both late and safe, I wish that we had allowed more time on our itinerary.

Monday, July 26

"Look, Michael, a caribou king!"

"What?" I asked in sleepy, groggy confusion.

"Look, a caribou drinking—at the lake right outside the tent!"

I opened my eyes. "Oh, yeah."

I looked at my watch. Only 5:30 am. I could rest a bit more. We could get up at 6:00, and be on the water by 9:00.

Only a few moments later, and my watch read 7:30. No wind. Maybe we'd have a calm day. I prepared breakfast quickly on the stove, and we paddled onto the lake at 9:40 am in perfectly calm weather. The ripples from paddles and canoe produced the only waves in the entire water kingdom of Aberdeen Lake.

Without wind, we glided easily across the mouths of bays

and inlets. Without being required to trace their much longer perimeters to avoid wind and waves, we covered distance two-to-three times more quickly.

A slight breeze sprang up from the NNE just before lunch on a fine sandy beach. As at yesterday's sandy beach, no biting bugs harassed us. In our brief experience on these lakes, mosquitoes and the small black flies much prefer cobblestone beaches or vegetated shore lines.

After a relaxing lunch for the second successive day, we again found ourselves paddling in calm conditions. We travelled with pleasure and joy across Aberdeen Lake's beautifully blue, clear waters. So very unlike the previous two days.

Just before reaching camp, we accidentally fell into our first argument of the journey. Like most disagreements between couples, the argument developed rapidly and unexpectedly from an innocent discussion. For us, the controversy erupted while looking at the maps.

"I think we're about here now, Kathleen. What do you think?"

"I don't know. It's not possible to be certain with all these bays along the shoreline."

"Don't you see that peninsula across the lake? We're right opposite it."

"You can't be so sure. They all look the same."

"If you refuse to see, then I don't want to talk about it."

We paddled the final 20 minutes in dejected, sorry silence.

We stopped at a white, fine-sand beach to camp. A beautiful decision. No wind, no biting or swarming bugs, 26 degrees, and only 4:00 pm! We heated two kettles of water on the stove, one to wash ourselves, the second to wash our clothes. We then luxuriated in sun-bathing, skin warmed by the sand and sun. We moved freely without confining, hot clothes. We breathed calmly, liberated from the harassment of insects. Without doubt, the most comfortable afternoon so far. It's hard to believe that only 48 hours ago we were cold, fatigued, and lost.

Our tentative schedule lists tomorrow as a rest day. We've agreed, however, to paddle if the weather remains calm. We'd be foolish to sit on the shore when paddling is so much easier and more productive when the wind has forgotten all about you.

The lake is beautiful on this calm, clear day. We easily paddled the distance planned for today; so, when we approached a white-sand beach in early afternoon, we stopped without hesitation and set up camp. During two bug-free hours, we undressed and washed, relaxing in the freedom from clothes, and from the pressure to achieve distance. Today we experienced our first harsh words of the trip, provoked mostly by fatigue, which reaffirmed our decision to stop, even though we could have accomplished many kilometres more. We expect to paddle tomorrow, if the calm holds, even though our itinerary indicates a designated rest day.

Tuesday, July 27

When we approached camp yesterday afternoon, the tail and dorsal fin of a large lake trout broke the water's surface, and I instantly hungered to catch another fish. I attempted a few casts after we washed, with no success. Hoping later to catch one for dinner, I walked farther down the shore line before noticing that sand had fouled the reel's mechanism. Back to camp for shepherd's pie and to disassemble and clean the reel for another attempt in the morning.

I awoke late, at 7:30 am. The weather was calm, and I felt an urgency to put on the water. We have to get to Baker Lake. I also wanted fish for breakfast. Ten casts with no action. I leaned the pole against a rock, and organized all the items for breakfast. I set the bag of dry bannock on a rock, and measured out a three-quarter cup of water. If I poured water into the bannock mix, I would be committed to preparing breakfast. I would no longer be able to fish. I set the cup aside, and placed a pot of tea water on the stove.

Back to the point to try for that breakfast fish. Seven casts later the fish struck! It appeared to be a nice lake trout—about 35 cm long. It should make a perfect-sized meal for two canoeists. I felt unusually hungry, though. During the trout's third run towards deeper water, I decided I should try to catch a second fish, just to be sure we have enough for breakfast. The fish turned and swam toward shore, then darted away. The tension on the line disappeared. The trout disappeared. Bannock for breakfast seemed inevitable.

I returned to the stove and made the tea, staring at the bannock mix and the cup of water.

"Kathleen, I really want trout for breakfast. Maybe I can try just five more casts."

"Try ten."

After five casts, nothing. Feeling pressure to get to Baker Lake, I looked at Kathleen.

"You said I should try 10 casts, so I will."

Three casts later, the trout struck a second time. Again, the fish managed to escape the hook. I then completed my ten allotted casts without success.

"You know, Kathleen, each strike should earn an additional five casts."

"Yes, just like when you get a few nickels from the slot machine; you have to keep trying."

Three casts later, the 40-cm fish lay on the beach. Thirty minutes later we enjoyed a sumptuous trout breakfast.

As a youth, I fished fanatically. I loved just to catch them. The more the better; but now I always feel a bit sorry for them. I empathize with any creature that struggles to survive, to maintain its life. Although I'm not convinced a lake trout is a feeling, sentient being, I can't summarily discount the possibility.

On the water at 10:30 am, beneath a low cover of visually and emotionally confining clouds. Hues of grey dominated the landscape of water and sky. Numerous snow banks lined the narrow beach, persisting at the base of 10-m bluffs, in the lee of the prevailing north winds.

Suddenly, opposite the canoe, we saw a wolf stalking geese along the shore. The geese seemed doubly panicked, uncertain whether to flee to the water to escape the wolf, or to flee inland to escape our human threat. I put in a "j stroke" to turn the canoe away from shore, giving the geese more room to elude the wolf.

I wonder why humans, a very successful predator, nearly always sympathize with the prey when the predator is non-human. While fishing this morning, I certainly didn't want the trout to escape; but now I wished success for the geese rather than for the wolf.

Perhaps it's because, without weapons, humans are not the most powerful or fearsome predator. Perhaps, despite being sealed from the natural world by 20th century civilization, there remains, imbedded in our psyche, a lingering fear that we might fall prey or victim to bear, wolf, lion or venomous snake. Perhaps that fear provides a natural alliance with weaker, innocent prey, such as the geese, so vulnerable and so ill-prepared for a struggle to the death.

Late in the afternoon, still paddling in a sombre, grey world, we landed on an island in a cove at the tip of Peqetuaz Peninsula. We stood before two magnificent stone pillars.

From James Tyrrell's journal:

> *"Towards the east end (of Aberdeen Lake), other remarkable traces of Eskimos were seen in the shape of stone pillars, well and uniformly built, but for what purpose I confess I cannot tell."*

The common experiences we are sharing with the Tyrrells cer-

tainly enhance my enjoyment of our Barren Grounds adventure.

We now know that these pillars were commonly constructed by Inuit to guide caribou to cross rivers or lake-narrows, where they could more easily be ambushed and killed from kayaks. This Barren Grounds landscape is harsh and difficult. To survive here as a culture for 6,000 years certainly required ingenuity and perseverance. We saw one caribou today. To kill it for sport would be difficult for me. To kill it for survival would be easy and natural.

We unloaded the canoe at 7:30 pm, after 38 km of paddling. A very good day. We have completed Aberdeen Lake, and are a day ahead of schedule. Our campsite is poor. Rocky, low terrain. Wet and buggy. Weather permitting, we'll move on tomorrow, and look for a nicer spot at Qamanaarjuk Lake to enjoy our rest day.

After a trout breakfast, we took advantage of another calm day to complete Aberdeen Lake, and are now camped on a bay west of Schultz Lake. Paddling late in the chilly drizzle, we were never tempted to camp anywhere in this dull, blue-grey world. Fatigue selected this campsite for us; probably the worst site of our trip, in a jumble of rocks interspersed with wet, mossy low ridges. The quiet, sombre evening is unsettling. I don't expect to sleep well tonight.

Wednesday, July 28

"Why does it sound like a river outside?" I had awakened to the sound of flowing water.

"It's the rocks," answered Kathleen.

"I didn't know rocks made noise."

"You hear the sound of waves washing up on the beach."

"Oh."

Outside the tent, the temperature had dropped to 8 degrees, made colder by a brisk wind. Paddleable, but just barely. I still didn't like the campsite, so we hurried through breakfast and packing, and shoved out into the surf at 10:30.

Our direction of travel sent us mostly east across Qamanaugaq Bay. Naturally, the wind adjusted itself to blow from the east. Progress came slowly. Once again we tacked out-and-back along the shore, staying between the rolling troughs of open water and the breaking waves on the shallow bay.

All adverse situations seem to provide opportunities that would otherwise be lost. Because the wind and waves forced us to trace the shore line, we spotted an over-turned boat on a low, rocky ridge. Stopping to investigate, we found not only the boat, but also paddles, mugs, repair kit, fishing pole, tackle box, camp equipment and clothing. All these items had been placed carefully beneath the modern, but badly-weathered fishing boat.

The Inuit traditionally interred their dead in shallow, rock-covered graves, bordered by the deceased's worldly possessions. Kathleen and I assumed that we had chanced upon such a site, commemorating an Inuit death in the ancestral fashion.

After lunch, we cleared the north-extending spit marking the eastern boundary of Qamanaugaq Bay. Turning east, we directly confronted our unrelenting adversaries of wind and waves. Despite our strongest possible strokes, we barely managed to clear the point.

"If we can just get down this east-trending shore line a little bit, we can reach the lee protection afforded by the higher hills forming Illurjualik Narrows."

Good idea. A few minutes later, two huge troughs swept toward us. The first wave rolled underneath, lifting the bow to an angle of 30°, and sending the canoe sliding, along with my stomach, down the wave's backside into the trailing ridge of menacing, green water.

The canoe shuddered, wallowed and pitched, but stayed upright. I muttered something like "Holy moly!!" Kathleen commanded "Get to shore!"

"No need to yell at me. I'm already headed that way."

Two-thirty in the afternoon. Four hours of paddling to advance only 8 km. Beached for the day. In the tent at 4:00, drinking hot tea and enjoying our daily allotment of gorp. We were warm, dry, and cozy. Still, we felt disappointed to have gained so little for our efforts. We napped until 6:30 pm before getting up to prepare beef stir-fry. We felt uneasy and threatened by the 11-degree temperature with drizzling rain and a persistent, irritating wind. Perhaps tomorrow will be more successful.

We fell asleep in an eerie calm last night, but awoke to wind and rain. After paddling only 8 km, we were forced to shore, where our tent is now pitched, exposed to the brunt of the wind. I'm glad to be on shore. After rounding a point we took the full impact of the north wind and wallowed in the waves. Our landing skills were severely tested.

After a quick, 30-minute venture into the cold and wind for dinner, we snuggled back into the tent. Although we stopped at 2:30 this afternoon, and travelled only a short distance, we remain about 15 km ahead of schedule. Wind causes me to worry about when we will be able to paddle again, and whether the energy we expended today was worth the short distance gained. I hope tomorrow is a calm day.

Thursday, July 29

I awoke at 8:00 am, well rested, but still pinned down by the wind, which blew unceasingly throughout the night. Still plenty of time in the day, though. If calm weather arrives, even by noon, we can still reach today's destination. I stepped outside into the drizzle, and stared at the eastern horizon. A thin strip of blue lay beneath the dark mass of clouds. Maybe the storm will break in a few hours.

The wind blows stronger today, and the rain continues. I'm frustrated. We are capable of completing this trip on schedule, but today we'll make no progress due to events beyond our control. Because by nature I am very impatient and like to feel in control of all situations, today promised to be a very bad day. I resolved to try to live each moment, and not worry or try to determine what will happen next. Normally, I would have been anxiously listening to hear if the wind were abating. Normally, I would be perpetually peeking out of the tent to see if the horizon were becoming brighter. This time, however, I spent the day in the tent playing solitaire. I established some "Barren Grounds Records" for "Thirteena," and I continued to see each new record fall throughout the day.

Back in the tent to doze and daydream for the next two hours. Thoughts of Baker Lake. Will there be camping available? Will there be pizza? Will the hotels be very expensive? Most often, though, my quiet visions centred on home and my garden. Will the sweetpeas be blooming? Will the root weevils have defoliated my azaleas while I'm not there to conduct my nightly flashlight searches? Will the thyme and hen-and-chicks have overgrown the stepping stones? Will this wind ever stop? Will we ever reach Baker Lake?

By 10:30 am, I became impatient with being imprisoned in the tent, and escaped for a hike along the adjacent ridge. Eight degrees—strong winds driving a stinging rain. Grey skies merging with cold tundra. Waves racing each other to disappear in foam on the sandy beach. The Barren Grounds were at their summertime best.

I boiled tea water while Kathleen rehydrated beef jerky stew for dinner. We willingly re-entered our tent-cell at noon for a dry, granola brunch. Not exactly eggs Benedict; but sufficient to continue our wait for calm weather and a departure for Baker Lake.

By 5:30 pm, we abandoned the faint hope of paddling today. No panic yet for reaching Baker Lake. We're only 20 km behind schedule, and our itinerary for tomorrow lists a rest day. We can easily catch up if we're blessed with good weather.

We are warm and dry in our tent, but must leave our shelter to cook if we want a hot supper. We have had only tea and granola so far today. In most accounts of early exploration found in Farley Mowat's book Tundra, *no food was distributed on days when poor weather forced stoppage of travel. No provisions could be wasted on days when work was not accomplished. My storm-bound day was certainly more enjoyable than those of the early explorers. During the rain, Michael went outside to make tea for us. I never once had to leave the tent during today's nasty weather.*

At 6:30 pm the rain stopped, and the wind slackened a short time later. Outside it had warmed to 11 degrees, and the southeast-facing hills across the water glowed faintly golden with sunlight penetrating the clouds. Still too cold and threatening to cook dinner outside. Instead, we decided on a snack party in the tent. Food catered by Kathleen. Tea, beef jerky, peanut butter on rye bread, prunes and our daily gorp. An excellent, easy meal.

Michael and I have developed a gauge to determine if the wind is too strong to paddle. If bugs are out, we can paddle; if not, canoeists must stay put. Despite the nuisance of the bugs, their adaptation during wind is entertaining: to survive, they must cling to the leaves of plants. The wind seems a much greater problem for them than for us. Around 8:00 pm, a dozen airborne mosquitoes gathered on the vestibule door netting. A beautiful harbinger regarding calming conditions. Maybe tomorrow we will escape this campsite.

Friday, July 30

My ears awoke shortly after 4:00 am to a wonderful sound. Silence. No tent flapping. No wind. Silence. I jubilantly dressed and stepped outside.

"Ow!"

Four degrees. Cold, but not as cold as yesterday's wind. Not cold enough to kill the mosquitoes, although they seemed dazed, and easy to slap into oblivion.

We savoured our bannock, which we missed yesterday, and paddled away from the beach at 7:00. Our earliest start yet. We intend to cover distance.

The morning was absolutely beautiful. A slight east breeze maintained crisp, fall-like conditions. The symphony of loons, sandhill cranes and herring gulls rose in full, joyous concert after two days of wind. Scores of misty columns of black flies rose as armies from the shore line. The mosquitoes might be dozy, and fall might have arrived; but bug season continued, as the breeze blew innumerable flies into the path of our canoe.

While riding the current in Illurjualik Narrows, we saw a pure white wolf on the left bank. Still a puppy, it broke into a bounding gait 100 m from the gaggle of geese it pursued. The geese escaped in a frenetic frenzy, and the wolf stared at the disappearing quarry in bewilderment. The look on its face seemed to say: "Just how in the hell do I catch these things, anyway?"

We drift easily into Qamanaarjuk Lake, enveloped in autumnal silence. Four common loons enchant us with an extended performance. The call of the loon certainly must be the quintessential sound of the Canadian wild. We stop to listen, to absorb the sound as it reverberates off the surrounding hills and glides musically back to us along the lake surface. This is certainly going to be a stunning day.

At 10:00 am we began to cross an open section of water on the east side of the peninsula. The wind had tricked us, and resumed its attack at the half-way point. We reached the shore with effort. No real risk, but still much too close to my comfort threshold.

We spent the next six hours in continued battle with our very familiar antagonist, but reached Schultz Lake at 1:30, and put in at a lovely, sheltered cove at 4:00 pm. A good day. We saw Inuit tent rings and fire hearths on Qamanaarjuk Lake. We encountered three muskoxen and one caribou, and completed 37 km aided by the current in Illurjualik Narrows and Aggattalik Narrows.

Our large-grained sand beach presented a new flower: an Arctic poppy. Our tent is situated perfectly. A view of 10 m out the front door to a gurgling stream, and the same distance out the back door to the now gentle waves of the lake lapping up onto the shore. The evening is calm and sun-filled. The Barren Grounds are again beautiful; but they are so moody and utterly unpredictable.

Here I sit in the sun. We began paddling this morning at 7:00 am, in calm clear weather. We made good time; but at about 10:00, the wind came up and hasn't quit yet. The east wind blew mostly in our faces; and when we arrived at Schultz Lake, very large waves swept toward our position on the western shore. It is difficult, emotionally and physically, to paddle in the wind. The water in these lakes is frigid. A swamping could kill us. To play it safe, we follow the shoreline, which often triples the distance we must paddle. It is tiring, but we made good distance and are now ahead of our itinerary. We are approximately 65 km from Aleksektok rapids. Only 65 km of lake travel remaining before the last stretch of river into Baker Lake. Hopefully, this is also the last 65 km that we will be affected by the wind.

When I started this adventure, I didn't fully appreciate that we would have to paddle and work as hard as we have. Much of our trip has been on large bodies of wind-blown water. Even though I enjoy being in this big country with just the two of us, it would be nice, sometimes, to have more hands for camp chores.

Building camp becomes more tiring each day. First, we have to find a suitable site, and this has been difficult the last few days. Then we must lift everything out of the boat, portage all gear to the campsite, make dinner, do the dishes, clean up and pack everything away. Only then can we retire for the evening.

Our tent has sheltered us very well, both from the wind and the rain. We feel very cozy with our pillows and therm-a-rests. I'm glad I purchased my overbag, even though the weather hasn't been cold enough to require it. I use the overbag like a blanket, which is more comfortable for me than the mummy bag. In many ways, our tent provides a reliable nest, to which we can retreat for security and warmth, no matter how hard we toiled during the day, and no matter how anxiously I may anticipate tomorrow.

Saturday, July 31

I stood on the shore at 7:00 am, fishing pole in hand. I had promised fish for breakfast, confident because of the tributary delivering food to waiting lake trout or grayling. The small bay was very shallow, though; only about 35 cm deep at the distance I could cast. Too shallow for fish; its rocky bottom would most likely ensnare my spinner.

Oh well, a promise must be attempted to be kept.

"Crum." Snagged on the first cast. I jerked quickly to free the lure. "Hey, it's a fish!"

The trout escaped near shore, but my optimism had been renewed. A second cast produced a second fish. A 30-cm lake trout. Another delicious breakfast.

While enjoying breakfast tea, we studied the maps and again noted the cluster of buildings indicated on the north shore of Schultz Lake. Brochures describing the recreational opportunities in the Keewatin District of the Northwest Territories confirmed that a fishing lodge existed here. About a week ago I began thinking that we could get coffee at the lodge, to vary our usual fare of tea. Three days ago I began to think "Heck, why should we get just coffee? If it's a lodge, we can get blueberry pie to go with our coffee!"

After breakfast, we prepared ourselves to become guests. We changed into our freshest clothes—we brushed our teeth for the second time that morning. Feeling appropriately prepared we set out for the lodge, and less than 60 minutes later gained our first view of the cluster of plywood buildings that stood shrouded in the silent, morning mist. We eagerly walked up the beach, only to find the lodge still boarded up from the winter, except for the cookhouse, which had apparently been broken into and ransacked by a grizzly bear. We paddled away, very disappointed to miss our blueberry pie and coffee, but content to know that we still remained alone in our Barren Grounds.

The ensuing canoeing day, highlighted by reaching our northern-most point at 64°48', seemed quite tedious. Hard paddling into a slight breeze in the morning. Easy paddling in calm conditions after lunch. By 4:00 that afternoon, my butt ached no matter how I positioned myself. To drift in moving water, would be such a relief.

We pitched camp on a tundra ridge at five o'clock. Thirty-two km completed. We'll certainly make Baker Lake now, almost no matter what tricks the wind may still spring upon us. I have mixed feelings tonight. The trip seems about over. This may well be the last night we ever spend as the only people camped at a large, silent, tundra lake.

The lake and western sun are visible from the tent door. Two muskoxen stand on the nearby ridge. They occasionally look apprehensively in our direction, but otherwise graze in pastoral, bovine, placidness. I'm looking forward to moving water, where the wind will exert less control over our destiny; however, I will miss these lakes, particularly at times like this, when the resting water can be so very tranquil and alluring.

We've made it to the Schultz Lake Peninsula. We are within a day of moving water, where we expect the wind to be considerably less debilitating. It is very calm and quiet tonight, except for the hum of mosquitoes. We're camped above a ridge of rocks pushed up on the shore by moving ice. As we climbed over the bank this afternoon, I stooped to appreciate the pink display provided by a large mat of river beauties. Many other flowers, including Arctic poppies, also adorned the bits of turf interspersed between the river-bank boulders. Up on the tundra ridge, the graceful floral plumes of mountain avens indicated that another Arctic summer was coming to an end. Two muskoxen graze quietly nearby. I can see them from the tent as I write.

We enjoyed fruit cake after dinner. Michael, particularly, has looked forward to this sweet dessert; and he doesn't even like fruit cake!

Today, as on other occasions, Michael told me we were about 20 minutes away from some landmark. I know 20 minutes means close, but actually arriving at the location is what counts for me. Michael brought a watch, but I didn't. It's difficult to tell the time of day simply by judging the quality of light in the sky; but knowing the time is not important to me. What matters is the distance travelled or the chores accomplished. We eat about one hour after arriving at camp. We leave camp about three hours after getting up. That is, we accomplish tasks in the time required to do them.

Michael caught another fish for breakfast. He left the head and entrails on the shore, and they were quickly eaten by a herring gull. The gull then sat and waited all through breakfast, and watched us from the shore while we packed. I guess the gull expected Michael to catch more fish for it.

I've truly enjoyed the relationship we've developed with all these tundra birds, which appear so completely unconcerned by our presence. We have paddled past Arctic terns sitting nonchalantly on rock points. Yellow-billed loons have landed calmly alongside our canoe. Terns and gulls commonly visit our camp to inspect our gear and to observe our activities. Smaller birds, such as American tree sparrows, semi-palmated plovers and Lapland longspurs, land near our camp, to sit on rocks or sand, seemingly just to say "hello."

Even though birds have journeyed here to reproduce in the short summer, I have the feeling that they are also on vacation. We seem to be sharing our vacations together. We also seem to be sharing the same feeling of safety and security. Although this land is demanding, Michael, the birds and I feel safe. Light persists long into the night, and the spacious Barrens are relatively empty of wild predators and human threats.

Sunday, August 1

Down to the river to catch a trout for breakfast. This time I take the frying pan in which to carry the fillets back to camp. Again I face a shallow, rocky shore line. Twenty casts, a dozen snags, one broken spinner. Back to camp to fill the frying pan with bannock.

We sit digesting a leisurely breakfast in the sun and calm. Conversation of reaching moving water. Kathleen reads a chapter of a book written by Clara Vyvyan, a British woman who travelled Great Slave Lake with her female companion in 1925. From there, these two adventurers descended the Mackenzie River to Aklavik, hired two guides to lead them up the Rat River to the height of land, and then descended the Porcupine River by themselves, past Old Crow, to the Yukon River. Their daring and courage, particularly for two women in the 1920s, far exceeds any of our exploits on this five-week holiday.

Vyvyan's book is a pleasure to read. Her description of Great Slave Lake simply, yet eloquently captured the grandeur and majesty of these lakes at rest. Kathleen often stopped reading, to compose herself, moved by the lyrical beauty of the words and the waterscapes before us.

> "I was alone again with that stillness emanating from sky and water, that magic stillness of the north, which is not the quiet of a little thing too weak to strive or cry, but the breath of a power brooding over all." - *Vyvyan*

We set out at 9:30 am in search of the outlet. Down the west side of Schultz Lake Peninsula, the wind blew at our backs. We rounded the point heading north, into the wind. "These waves aren't so big. There's not even whitecaps. We can easily handle this."

I left these thoughts unspoken, as the wind may be listening. I only hope the wind can't read my mind.

The island on the southeastern tip of the peninsula proved impassable on the landward side, so we paddled out into the channel and wind. Clearing the island, we found ourselves in waves breaking on the island shoals. Quartering into the breakers, we intended to lunch when we touched the mainland in a few minutes.

The shore line, however, receded from our quartering direction, which we needed to maintain to prevent the waves from striking us broadside. The more we paddled, the farther we distanced ourselves from shore. The wind now intensified, making our position more precarious than we wished. This combination of island, wind and receding shore line had occurred on many occasions. Too often to be mere coincidence. I'm convinced that this land-and-water juxtaposition has been conceived by the wind to lure careless canoeists into more vulnerable positions.

Eventually we accepted the broadside blows, and headed straight to the beach. While waiting for the soup to steep, I took a compass reading, and discovered we were directly opposite the point of a bay where the Schultz Lake outlet should lie. Five km of open water in a stiff breeze.

I'm sure that other people would have attempted the crossing, and likely could reach the opposite shore 99% of the time. That remaining 1% of the time, however, when the wind unexpectedly throws 1-2 metre breakers at your 16-foot canoe, is too much of a risk. Only three outcomes are possible. With luck, the shore is reached safely, without mishap. With no luck, the canoeists swim to shore, frightened, cold and wet. With bad luck, a mid-crossing capsize proves fatal.

Kathleen and I are on holiday. The risk of an open crossing, with no tangible benefit, is unwarranted. It's precisely this situation that we believed could be problematic and contentious when travelling with other people. There will always be someone who accepts the risk, foolishly or calculatingly. In these situations, peer pressure often encourages the entire group to accept the same risk.

Kathleen and I continued up the peninsula, seeking the shorter 2-km crossing indicated on the map. I steered the canoe as far from the west bank as seemed safe, to provide a head start to the eastern shore when the crossing seemed appropriate. After 45 minutes, I posed the question.

"Do you think we can make it?"

"I think so."

Ten minutes of hard stroking and we turned south along the east bank, the final crossing of the lake section of our journey completed. The wind would no longer pose such a threat to progress or peace of mind.

After only two-and-a-half hours from lunch, we entered the rock-strewn bay containing the outlet. For what seemed like the 82nd time, no obvious outlet existed. Once again, the compass proved valuable, pointing 40 degrees to where the outlet should take us from Schultz Lake. Although no current seemed to flow in that direction, we trusted the compass, which had been remarkably accurate, even at this latitude.

We reached moving water at 4:00 pm, and ran the outlet rapids on the inside bend, where two attorneys from California were fishing from shore. We shared conversation, and talked of Baker Lake. Later in the evening, their guide motored up-river in a boat, with a companion and a dog. We seem to have reached civilization.

I'm pleased to be off the lakes, and am now very tired. The tension of worrying about reaching our goal has dissipated completely. Only 90 km to go. Only one rapid, and perhaps one portage, separates us from Baker Lake. Perhaps that's why my satisfying feeling of isolation terminated the moment the river's current bore us down to the attorney's camp.

We're off the lakes! We are camped tonight on moving water with the roar of rapids in our ears. Tomorrow we will come to our last major obstacle, Aleksektok Rapids, about one hour down stream. It's funny how things are—and then they are not—with no transition to ease the change. Last night we were in the wilderness— just Michael and I. Today we are not, and won't truly be again on this trip. This morning, overhead, we saw a plane with wheels for landing at airports, not pontoons for landing on water. When we rounded the first bend in the river to stop at our expected camping place, two men were there already, fishing. The men were transported here by motor boat from Baker Lake in 3.5 hours; so, even though I expect we'll be alone two or three more nights, we know we're easily within reach of other people and civilization.

Our lives on the Barrens have changed so suddenly. At lunch we still hadn't made the crossing from the peninsula extending into Schultz Lake. The wind was strong, and we were faced with a paddle of many kilometres up the peninsula and down the other side to make a safe crossing. What if the wind became stronger, though? Might we still be on the other side, perhaps winded for days? We are now on moving water, and within one or two days of Baker Lake. We should arrive several days ahead of schedule.

Monday, August 2

Feeling elated at reaching moving water, we slept in, and enjoyed another dawdling breakfast of lake trout. So wonderful to catch breakfast so easily on nearly a daily basis. We chatted a bit with the attorneys, who had broken camp at 9:00 am, and now waited for their guide to return from Schultz Lake to take them down-river, three hours to Baker Lake.

The guide, his companion and the dog returned shortly before noon, and all seven of us clustered on the shore. The Thelon seemed very populous. We fired several questions at the guide.

"Where's the campground in Baker Lake?"

"How far does the current extend into Baker Lake?"

"Where's the portage trail around Aleksektok Rapids?"

After five weeks of making all our own decisions, only one day of civilization and people began to erode our independence. The attorneys, guide, companion and dog left shortly after noon, leaving us behind on the beach. They'll be in Baker Lake in three hours. We'll be there in three days.

Suddenly we felt as though we were canoeing and camping on the Trans Canada Highway; a pointless activity. Our trip was over. We no longer felt that we lived in a pristine, wilderness landscape. Why, then, must we still continue as though we did? No choice, that's why.

We reached Aleksektok Rapids at 1:30 pm, and by 3:30 concluded that a 2-km portage was necessary. High, standing waves in the centre channel; pour-overs throughout; diagonal, curling waves on both shorelines. Probably runnable, but not guaranteed.

We were very irritated. Our trip was over. In a perverse way, we had been excited and challenged by the Thelon Canyon portage. The portage route that now stretched before us represented only an imposition. Our adventure had ended at the outlet of Schultz Lake, the moment we exchanged greetings with the attorneys. We had celebrated our success with two glasses of Sunday brandy last night instead of our usual trip-allotment of one glass. I haven't even taken any photographs today. Our journey was over, and yet we must now begin our second-longest portage of the trip. We were very irritated.

Only two kilometres. Just one more obstacle. Kathleen and I carried the white buckets and our day packs to the end of the portage, scouting the best route as we went: in-and-out of the boulder field, through the boggy swamp, past the dead gull, and over the rise down to the river. Kathleen had been feeling ill all day and we decided she should stay in camp to set up the tent and prepare dinner while I retrieved the rest of our gear. Back over the rise, past the dead gull, through the boggy swamp, and in-and-out of the boulder field brought me back to the canoe packs. I loaded as much as I possibly could carry on my back, and then attached some smaller packs to my heavy load. I then re-traced my steps back to camp: in-and-out of the boulder field, through the boggy swamp, past the dead gull, and over the rise down to the river. Kathleen handed me a snack, and cut some mole skin to place over the blisters on my very hot and weary feet.

I now returned for the canoe: back over the rise, past the dead gull, through the boggy swamp, and in-and-out of the boulder field brought me back to the last portage load of our adventure. I lifted the canoe over my head, and rested the carrying yoke on my shoulders. Half way through the boulder field, my shoulders began to ache, and I flung the canoe to the ground. A few minutes later I was off once more, but stopped again when I reached the end of the boulder field. My body, although hardened after 5 weeks on the river, now seemed to rebel at carrying any more loads. I stared at the canoe. I surveyed the landscape.

M. Pitt

Commemoration of a drowning at Aleksektok Rapids.

I took a deep breath, but was barely able to lift the canoe onto my shoulders. I vowed to carry it until I reached the dead gull, but searing pain in my shoulders, plus the blisters on my feet forced me to lower the canoe to the ground half way through the boggy swamp. I breathed heavily as I looked around the tundra. No sign of the rise, beyond which lay our camp, dinner, and Kathleen. No sign of any humans to help me. I seemed alone in the oppressive afternoon heat. Millions of bugs swarmed about me, as I stood ankle deep in the tepid, boggy water. I looked at the canoe. I surveyed my surroundings. I looked at the canoe. My mind focussed on the task before me, as the following single, satisfying emotion permeated my existence: "My God, this is beautiful!"

By 8:30 pm we had carried all the gear to the end of whitewater, had pitched camp, and were relaxing with tea after the chili and cornbread dinner. The river is blasting along at least 10 km/hour. Maybe we'll be in Baker Lake tomorrow. I hope so. These bugs are really beginning to irritate me.

It seems the trip as we knew it has ended. It just feels different—not as nice. To avoid the two-kilometre Aleksektok rapids, we had to portage through hummocky, boggy, wet country. The bugs were terrible. We are camped in the only semi-flat, dry spot available; even then, we pitched our tent on rocks.

The river has picked up a very strong current, and we are concerned about what conditions will be like between here and Baker Lake. Yesterday, the attorneys said that no more rapids lay below the portage, but that several narrows constricted the river into large waves and rough water. The Tyrrells wrote about difficult sections, through which the Inuit showed them the best chutes. Until now, we have accepted all adversities in stride; but somehow, the uncertainties we now face seem different. We have received first-hand information, and no longer have the opportunity for personal discovery. The current is strong enough that we could complete the 80 km to Baker Lake in one day. I wish this (these) last day(s) could feel good, as the trip has been so wonderful.

August 2—August 3
Aleksektok Rapids to
Baker Lake

August 1   Aleksektok
Rapids
August 2

August 3
Baker
Lake

N

TRIAL AND VICTORY

Tuesday, August 3

Our tent had been pitched on gravel along the river bank, on a 20-degree slope. As such, we claimed the best campsite for kilometres around. I slept fitfully all night, concerned about the tumultuous river between us and Baker Lake. The Thelon, after five weeks of meandering, usually with no current, suddenly seemed desperately eager to reach its mouth at Baker Lake.

I arose at 7:00 am to brooding skies and brooding, grey, boggy tundra. No hint of sun to warm the brisk, southerly wind. The air was cold at 12° C, and the water even colder at 7° C. After breakfast, we hiked back along the ridge to photograph Aleksektok Rapids and plants. Apparently, when we weren't looking, autumn had sneaked into the Arctic landscape. The blueberries were now ready for eating, and the fruit of the red bearberry had turned the tundra floor a scarlet colour.

Back on the cobblestone beach, we loaded the canoe, which was difficult to restrain in the sliver-eddy beside the very swift water. The river was larger and faster than anything we had ever paddled. We spoke apprehensively about the river's two remaining obstacles. One waited for us about 20 minutes downstream, while the second, an island, lay 18 km away. Both spots constricted the flow of water, likely creating even higher standing waves.

"Are you ready, Kathleen?"

"I guess so."

We shot into the current, and sped quickly away from our rocky, river-side camp. We reached the first constriction almost instantly. After a brief scouting from shore, we climbed back into the canoe, and easily avoided the large haystacks by ferrying to river-left. *This isn't so bad, and we're making great progress! We proceeded down-river, gaining confidence and comfort in the boils and large waves.*

After 45 minutes we had completed 10 km with very little paddling. Mostly, we merely sat in the canoe, and maintained our anticipatory high braces to keep the canoe parallel with the current, and to prevent a sideways entry into the wallowing troughs. We reached the island in an hour and 20 minutes. Again, we easily skirted the large haystacks on the outside bend, although the deflecting boils and waves from the inside bend provided some concern.

We were through, though. The last obstacle! Lots of current. We're averaging about 13 km/hour. This is actually fun! We spent the next few hours following the fast water from outside bend to outside bend. After lunch the rain began, and we paddled in silence, heads down, hoping vainly for sun. At least there's no more obstacles. Even the whirlpools and boils in this section of the river aren't too bad.

I really dislike whirlpools and boils. It's like paddling in cotton candy; there's no substance. The canoe seems suspended, with the paddle providing little purchase. Yet, as with sticky cotton candy, the canoe becomes entangled, drawn in a variety of directions, each of which melts into a new set of whirlpools and boils.

By 4:00 pm we had covered 60 km. *A cold drizzle began mid-day, and intensified in late afternoon. We were about 20 km and 3 hours from Baker Lake, riding a swift current, when we agreed to push on rather than camp one last night on the river. Good camping spots had not been evident along the high, soggy banks, and we were wetter than we'd been on the entire trip.*

All day I had paddled with my white-water paddle, in case I suddenly needed to make forceful strokes. The fast water intimidated me, and I continually gazed ahead for evidence of rapids. On this very straight section of the Thelon, I was often fooled by the white horizon-line. In late afternoon, I again thought I saw white, frothing water; but, peering through my rain-stained glasses, I again discounted the potential threat.

We approached the 2-km S-bend that emptied into a wide, shallow section of the river just upstream from its delta that drains into Baker Lake. Suddenly the boils and whirlpools became larger, and decidedly uncomfortable.

"Why are these here now? I don't see any reason for them."

"I don't know, Michael."

"Do you see rapids down there?"

"No, do you?"

"I don't know. It looks a bit white, and I think I can hear rapids."

"It's probably just a tributary spilling over rocks. You know how loud they can sound."

"Yeah, that's right. Let's go."

We entered the right-trending portion of the S-bend and immediately wished we hadn't. *Only then, and too late, we realized that the bend constricted the river into enormous waves.* Standing waves nearly two metres high deflected off the left bank, and swirled toward us in an ominous series of whirlpools. *Our only hope to avoid capsize would be to hold our boat steady in the circulating boils without being dragged across the eddy line into the powerful reversal-current. My body went completely ice cold. I felt I might not have the strength to make the necessary strokes. I called into the wind "God be with us. Please God, be with us."*

"I'm scared, Michael."

"I don't like this either."

We braced, heading right, toward river-centre, to escape the diagonal, curling tongues of green and white. My breathing came in short, staccato bursts. This looks bad.

Ahead, we could see the river channel bending back towards the left. The river surged toward this outside bend, and slammed into the cliff face. Our canoe sped toward the cliff, where the water piled up in 2.5-m-high standing waves. Adrenaline and fear fought for control of my body and mind. To continue right meant certain capsize. In silence, we struggled to reverse our direction. Kathleen drew left. I swept right. The canoe turned sluggishly toward the inside bend on river-left.

Still in silence, we powered diagonally across deep haystacks created by the current deflecting off the point around which the river narrowed and veered sharply left. Immediately beyond the point, a powerful reversal eddy re-entered the main current in a mountainous ridge of breaking, irregular waves.

"Oh, most terrible expletive!" Five weeks on the journey, and we're going to die three hours from Baker Lake. Most of all, though, I feared the humiliation of knowing what our fellow canoe club members in Vancouver would say about our self-inflicted demise: "They committed the worst sin of wilderness canoeing —entering a blind canyon without scouting first. They should have known better."

We braced against the waves as we guided the canoe toward the eddy line below the ridge of water. Struggling against the opposing currents, we alternately powered and braced to hold our parallel position between the dangerous reversal on our left and the impossible waves to our right. Fear continued to assault my being. Would we ever reach the end of this canyon?

Finally, the broad opening beyond the S-bend appeared. I think we're going to live! *Fear had now sapped all my energy. I knew I couldn't paddle through another rapid. All I wanted was to get to shore, but the strong current of the wide Thelon continued flushing us down-river. From the map Michael knew the river soon opened up into its delta, and that we had already passed through the worst of the rapids. I hadn't studied this section of the map, and didn't know that we needed only to brace against the haystacks created by moving water emptying into the delta. I accepted Michael's advice, though, to keep paddling until we reached calm water.*

The river ejected us through the gap, and we rode the dissipating haystacks to river-left, where we beached the canoe for a gorp break and the pleasure of standing on land. I felt genuinely pleased to be alive. That was the most scared I have ever been in my life.

Back in the boat, after a sausage and gorp snack, we rounded Hornet Point at 6:30 pm, and paddled easily toward the tight-clustered collection of buildings comprising Baker Lake.

In the still, grey evening, water seemed to stretch beyond the horizon. Only a sliver of land was evident to our left. We paddled along this left bank, and eventually gained our first view of the town of Baker Lake. From our vantage point, there seemed no movement or sound; but as we drew closer, life became evident—a man tended his fishing nets on the shore. We touched shore at 7:30, just under nine hours—eight on the water—to complete 80 km. The fisherman, an Inuk, held our boat against the shore while we relaxed in our bow and stern positions.

"Did you see many caribou?" the fisherman asked.

"No, only about a dozen, all singles."

"Not many caribou this year," he said. "Where did you come from?"

"Lynx Lake."

"Long trip. Bet you saw lots of mosquitoes."

"Yeah. It was a hard trip. We're tired. We've come all the way from Aleksektok Rapids today. The current was pretty fast."

"High water right now," replied the fisherman.

"Do you know where the campground is?"

The man looked around. "There used to be a picnic table over there, but it's gone now."

Kathleen asked about hotels.

"The Baker Lake Lodge is not as expensive as the Iglu. Closer too. Just up this hill," as he pointed to a new building only a few hundred metres away.

We thanked him for the advice, and for offering to store our canoe on the beach in front of his house.

Our appearance at the lodge, dripping wet and still wearing our PFDs and spray skirts, obviously surprised the hotel proprietor; but a room was available, and we moved in moments later. As Michael portaged the packs up from the canoe, I began hanging wet equipment to dry. I soon filled the room, and spread the rest of our gear in the hall and on the small porch. "How did we fit all this into the canoe, when it won't even fit into a hotel room?"

We're now at the Baker Lake Lodge. A hot bath, a bed, brandy, and no bugs. I am very satisfied to have journeyed these past 5 weeks. I'm equally satisfied to have reached our destination.

I'm sitting in a bed, surrounded by drying clothes, packs, and

K. Pitt

Hoare Point—our first tundra lake camp.

tent. *I've soaked in a hot bath, and am protected from the mosqui-*
toes in our warm, dry room. We have accomplished our goal
embarked on so many weeks ago at Lynx Lake. Why, then, am I
not exhilarated or even content?

Since the last day on Schultz Lake, there has been a sadness
within me. Our trip was ending too soon. Last night my mood was
intensified by worry about the strong current evident as we scouted
the river below Aleksektok Rapids.

Shaken by our experiences in the S-bend rapid, we are sipping
brandy while assessing our feelings. My parents congratulated us
when we called them tonight. Perhaps, with time, the trip will feel
more like an accomplishment. Tonight, though, I feel mostly loss.
Our special time alone together is over. Our special relationship with
the land, birds and animals is over. Maybe this moment is just part
of the natural cycle. It is fall, and even the birds will soon fly south,
leaving this vast land as empty as I feel tonight.

Wednesday, August 4

I arose at 7:00 am, and prepared our bannock breakfast on the porch of the hotel room. Five-week-old habits, particularly enjoyable habits, are changed only reluctantly. We look forward to tomorrow's bannock breakfast.

We spent the day touring Baker Lake, meeting new people. It's intriguing to learn how non-native people came to live in this Arctic community. Marie Bouchard, owner of Baker Lake Fine Arts And Crafts, arrived eight years ago to write a book about the starvation of Inuit during the 1950s. Ironically, she opened the store to prevent her own figurative starvation while pursuing her literary aspirations. Liz Kotelewetz arrived as a nurse over 20 years ago, and now manages the very delightful, spacious Baker Lake Lodge. She continues to administer to the community as social counsellor.

It's difficult to accept that our Barren Grounds canoe quest has ended. The anticipation of this journey has dominated my thoughts for 18 months. The splendor of solitude and isolation is not available in urban centres. Even in Baker Lake, civilization supersedes all. The sounds of mechanized travel, on ATVs, permeates the community, even though virtually all buildings can be reached in a 15-minute walk.

We watched the CBC news this evening, and were distressed to realize how incapable humans seem to be of solving their problems. All headlines remained unchanged since we left Vancouver seven weeks ago. War in Bosnia. Riots in South Africa. White police officers on trial for beating black motorist Rodney King. Prime Minister Campbell, condemned for giving Quebec special concessions, might call an election soon. The U.S. Congress might not pass the North American Free Trade Agreement. We have witnessed three Arctic seasons. The earth has revolved around the sun 40 times; but, all the while, humankind has remained at a standstill. Our home and garden beckon, but I wonder what will fill the void of freedom lost.

We gently eased out of our river routines today. Michael fired up the backpacking stove to make breakfast tea and bannock on the porch. There are no restaurants in Baker Lake. The Lodge provides one sitting for a family-style breakfast, which we declined in lieu of sleeping late.

We traversed the town, absorbing the atmosphere and searching for souvenirs. Many people in this friendly town were interested in our adventure. We purchased hand-made duffle and fur slippers for Mom, and a sweatshirt with an original Inuit silk screen for Dad. For my kitchen, I bought embroidered, duffle oven-mitts.

Our room is still littered with drying gear and equipment. Hopefully we can start packing up in the morning. We've spoken to Loon Air; weather permitting, they will retrieve us on Friday. The 900 km to Fort Smith is a long distance for a Cessna 185. I've been dreading the flight back to Fort Smith in the cramped little plane, and have been trying to determine a way to avoid it. But, if we want to take our canoe, the Cessna is our only choice.

I wore my anniversary earrings for the first time today, exactly one month after receiving them. That day in July, more than 900 km upstream from Baker Lake, doesn't seem so long ago. I haven't had much time yet to think back on our adventure. I'm sure we will reflect much more on our Thelon journey once we're home in Vancouver.

After dinner at the Lodge, we watched the CBC news, hoping for information regarding how well the Atlanta Braves were doing in their drive for a third-straight divisional title. As I watched and listened vainly for the baseball scores that never came, the main news items were reminiscent of the last news report we had heard six weeks ago. The world has continued on with its unrest, fear and violence, while we have lived in the freedom and simplicity of our Barren Grounds adventure.

Saturday, August 7

We spent our two-and-one-half days in Baker Lake in leisure-ly walks, attending to errands and business. Two trips to the

RCMP to inform them that we had arrived. Three visits to each of the four arts and crafts centres to select gifts for family, house-sitters, and work colleagues. For ourselves, to commemorate our Thelon River adventure, we purchased a pastel drawing by Simon Tookoomik, a Baker Lake Inuk. Writing postcards, buying stamps, frequenting the visitor's centre, and dinners at the lodge easily filled our time. Best of all, the vagaries of wind no longer dominated our senses and actions.

On Friday morning we called Loon Air in Fort Smith to confirm our flight that afternoon. After three unsuccessful attempts, the operator informed us that Loon Air's business number was no longer in service! Had they gone out of business, stranding us in Baker Lake? Not likely, we reasoned, and tried again an hour later. Our call now went through, and we learned that all lines had been knocked out by an electrical wind storm, and that our charter plane was already in the air.

Moments later, the Cessna 185 flew over the Baker Lake Lodge, and landed in front of the Northern Store. We scurried to our room, portaged the gear to the canoe, and paddled to the now-fuelled plane.

While we stood on the pontoon waiting to enter the cabin, two paddlers just in from the Kazan River walked across the beach to talk about Barren Grounds canoeing. They had arrived only hours before, and their faces literally glowed with enthusiasm and excitement. I envied them, as my own emotions were much less joyous. Perhaps now that we had paddled the Thelon River and its tundra lakes, simply by living one day at a time, the journey's very remarkable qualities seemed normal, commonplace and mundane. Perhaps the joy and sense of special accomplishment will come later.

As always before a flight, my heart beat faster and my stomach churned. I relaxed somewhat watching our pilot, Paul, inspect all the plane's checkpoints. Our depleted supplies allowed much more room for me to sit comfortably in the rear of the cabin, and I snuggled down amongst the packs. After a smooth take-off, we flew evenly over the tundra. Only one more take off and two more land-ings. We just might make it!

Paul took off easily into the north wind, and we banked south toward Fort Smith, our direction "locked in" by the global positioning system. Below, the Barren Grounds stretched endlessly, dominated by lakes and water courses. We flew silently across the unchanging landscape. Had we really traversed this open emptiness alone? Wow!

We crossed Dubawnt Lake, an immense body of water, purported by Paul to be as large as Massachusetts. A short time later we landed at Damant Lake for refuelling. The float plane coughed and wheezed, and sputtered against the shore next to the ubiquitous red-and-yellow fuel drums.

"Cracked fuel line," Paul remarked, with incredible nonchalance. "I'll try to fix it."

I watched nervously as Paul removed the front fuselage and unpacked his screw drivers and other tools.

"I could jerry-rig this to work, but I don't want to take a chance. I'll radio for help."

Michael and I wandered onto the esker, then back down into the trees -- a special treat for us after nearly six weeks on the Barrens. We settled in the shelter of a hill away from the strengthening winds. Our sausages, peanut butter, crackers and gorp made a good meal. Paul joined us after relaying a message to Fort Smith, through Yellowknife. As the afternoon lengthened into evening, we considered putting up the tent. Michael eagerly talked about catching fish for dinner. I was hoping not to be saved just yet, as I very much wanted to continue living in the Barren Grounds. All too soon, however, we heard the drone of the approaching rescue plane that would eventually carry us away, back to Fort Smith.

About 8:30 pm, a second Cessna 185 landed on Damant Lake. Dick, the manager and mechanic of Loon Air held the required replacement part in his hand, and he immediately began repairing the broken fuel line. The pilot, Don, greeted us enthusias-

tically, and pumped us for information about our adventures since he had left us at Lynx Lake on that warm afternoon in June.

After quickly completing the repair with a 50-cent piece of tubing, Dick suggested that Michael and I should travel in the "rescue" plane. I worried about flying in the now deepening dusk. Even though we couldn't make Fort Smith before nightfall, both pilots wanted to at least get off the Barrens. Thekulthili Lake, about 1 hour away, became our destination. Paul took off first, without incident. We followed, but soon passed the first plane, which was slowed by our canoe strapped to the pontoon. Although not yet legally night, the lake looked dark as Don flew low over the water surface, looking for rocks and shoals. Paul landed about 5 minutes later, and we all tied up to shore in front of a rustic fishing lodge.

Once our sleeping bags were spread on the bunks we enjoyed a beer, compliments of Dick and Loon Air. The rest of the evening passed quickly, as we listened to stories of flying and mishaps in this vast, empty land.

We awoke to a heavy mist hanging over the lake. As we drank our coffee, we stared toward the end of the lake, searching hopefully for signs that the fog may be lifting. Don and Paul studied the maps, looking for water routes above which they could fly safely. Don was ready when the far shore became visible, so we taxied down the lake and took off for Fort Smith.

The fog soon thickened, and I strained ahead to see potential obstacles that might suddenly emerge from the mist that now covered the land. Don banked sharply, and turned back and landed on a small, unnamed patch of water barely visible beneath the thickening mist. Another landing! Rocky, steep, well-treed banks surrounded this lake, contrasting sharply to the open tundra to which we had become so accustomed.

Don flew in fog only when he could see lakes, which provided potential emergency landings. He never flew in fog over land. We appreciated Don's cautious motto: "Never close the back door. When the Barrens bite, they bite hard."

We had violated Don's creed when we entered the S-bend without scouting, and without knowing beforehand that we could get off the river if necessary. We had closed the back door when we entered the canyon, and barely slipped through the front door before it slammed shut. We narrowly, and somewhat luckily, avoided being bitten very hard.

About an hour later, the ceiling lifted slightly, revealing the lake's far shore. After taking off for the second time this morning, the southern horizon continued to become brighter. Just before lunch we taxied up to the Loon Air float dock on Four Mile Lake. Paul didn't arrive with our gear and canoe until around 4:00 pm; he had been unable to leave the fishing lodge this morning, as the fog returned to Thekulthili Lake only moments after Don, Michael and I had flown away.

We returned to the Pelican restaurant for the pizza we'd been looking forward to since arriving in Baker Lake. After dinner Don, Paul and another young pilot joined us at our Fort Smith campsite for beer and more bush-pilot stories. The skill of these pilots had safely transported us to and from the Thelon River. It seemed fitting to end our adventure in their company.

RETURN

'Yet feet that wandering have gone, turn at last to home.'
- J.R.R. Tolkien, The Hobbit

It's good to be home, but I miss the river already. Despite being dominated by wind and water, we alone determined our daily activities. If the wind whipped up waves too high for paddling, we rested. If the river plunged through canyons or over ledges, we portaged. Other than for our self-imposed deadline of August 6 for reaching Baker Lake, time was interesting, but otherwise meaningless.

We had lived and travelled through an everlasting landscape. We had shared our journey with plants, birds, caribou, muskoxen, bears and wolves, all of us participating in the predictable progression of seasonal change. The concept of linear time, with beginning and end, is viewed by many native cultures as an artificial perspective. In reality, there is no beginning. There is no end. Seasonal cycles spin forever. As they always have. As they always will. Living within such cycles, time is irrelevant. Time can not be saved. Time can not be lost. Without a linear construct, time can not exist.

In Vancouver, time assumes nearly paramount importance. We arrived home on Wednesday evening, with four days to be ready for our commute beginning precisely at 7:06 on Monday morning. I spent Thursday and Friday tending to eight weeks of accumulated garden weeds and household chores. As I collected together the necessary gardening implements, I noticed a flat tire on the commuter car. No problem. I expected this, as the tire had been leaking slowly before we left. I wrestled the spare out of the trunk. It too was flat. Not too flat to drive, though. I inserted the key in the ignition. Click..click...click. Dead battery. A call to the BC Automobile Association instructed me to be ready in exactly 40 minutes.

Into the garden with hoe in hand. Ten minutes later Kathleen emerged from the laundry room with news that the dryer no longer produced heat. Back to the phone to contact the appliance store. The unseen voice told me they opened at 10:00, and might have replacement parts for our 20-year-old dryer.

On the river, all our equipment was functional and reliable, with virtually no moving parts. Self-sufficiency was blissfully easy. Alleged conveniences of civilization in Vancouver were frustratingly domineering by comparison. The phone rang demandingly. News of a house-warming party in the Fraser Valley. Drinks at 4:30 pm for dinner at 6:00.

The assembled guests expressed genuine interest in our Barren Grounds adventure. We basked in the 15 minutes of fame promised to all of us by Andy Warhol. Our fans ebbed and flowed during the evening, asking questions that invariably followed a predictable pattern.

"Did you see any bears?"

"Three."

"How close?"

"One was about from here to that far wall."

"Did you take a gun?"

"No, just cayenne pepper spray."

"Were the bugs bad?"

"They were horrible. Worse than I ever imagined they could be."

"How was the weather?"

"Variable. Wind—particularly wind. Sun and rain. No snow, though. Our coldest temperature was 4° C."

"How long was the trip?"

"Five-and-one-half weeks; 950 km. But it didn't really seem so long. You just live one day at a time no matter where you are. It's no different or longer than living in Vancouver for five-and-one-half weeks."

"Did you have an air drop for food?

"No, Kathleen dehydrated all our food, which was excellent. We even have food left over."

"Did you have a radio?"

"No, but we did take an EPIRB for emergencies."

All very logical questions, but all of them totally missing the essence of wilderness canoeing. When my thoughts drift back to our quest, they settle comfortably on the multitudes of geese that gave us constant companionship. I can still see us drifting toward shore, anxiously surveying the bank for suitable camping sites. I can still see us eating bannock on a sunny morning, gazing restfully over a lake equally at rest. I can still see the orange-spotted white petals of prickly saxifrage, growing delicately among the riverside cobbles at the Mary Francis River. I can still taste the tart fruit of the blueberry, growing modestly in a tangle of lichens above Aleksektok Rapids. And,

I can still remember lying in the tent pitched above Schultz Lake, listening to the hushed breath of absolute silence that reached out to us from beyond infinite, isolated tundra lakes and mountains.

Our most vivid memory, however, remains the enduring magic of living—as nomads—in Canada's isolated, northern landscape. Our freedom was exquisite and absolute. It was as though we were the only two people in the world, travelling through a natural landscape so vast that it still functions as it has since the days it was first created.

We can hardly wait to go again.

Lasting memories of the Finnie River from Lookout Point.

SELECTED READINGS

Burt, Page. 1991. *Barrenland Beauties*. Outcrop Ltd., Yellowknife, Northwest Territories. 246 pp.

Christian, Edgar V. 1937. *Unflinching: A Diary of Tragic Adventure*. John Murray, Ltd., London. Republished as Death in the Barren Ground. 1980. G. Whalley (ed.).

Hodgins, Bruce W., and Margaret Hobbs. 1985. *Nastawgan*. Betelgeuse Books, Willowdale, Ontario. 231 pp.

Kesselheim, Alan S. 1989. *Water and Sky: Reflections of a Northern Year*. Stoddart Publ. Co. Ltd., Toronto, Ontario. 311 pp.

Mason, Bill. 1988. *Song of the Paddle*. Key Porter Books Ltd., Toronto, Ontario. 186 pp.

McCreadie, Mary (ed.). 1995. *Canoeing Canada's Northwest Territories*. Canadian Recreational Canoeing Association, Hyde Park, Ontario. 194 pp.

McHugh, Gretchen. 1987. *The Hungry Hiker's Book of Good Cooking*. Alfred A. Knopf, New York. 286 pp.

Mowat, Farley. 1973. *Tundra*. McClelland & Stewart Inc., Toronto, Ontario. 467 pp.

Norment, Christopher. 1989. *In the North of Our Lives*. Down East Books, Camden, Maine. 248 pp.

Pelly, David. F. 1996. *Thelon: A River Sanctuary*. Canadian Recreational Canoeing Association, Hyde Park, Ontario. 202 pp.

Rossbach, George B. 1966. *By Canoe Down the Thelon River*. Beaver. Autumn:4-13.

Vyvyan, Clara C. 1961. *Arctic Adventure*. Owen, London, Eng. 172 pp.

Wilson, Ian, and Sally Wilson. 1992. *Arctic Adventures: Exploring Canada's North by Canoe and Dog Team*. Gordon Soules Book Publ. Ltd., West Vancouver, British Columbia. 246 pp.

THELON RIVER PROFILE

The Thelon River between Lynx Lake and Baker Lake includes three quite distinct paddling sections. The first section from Lynx Lake to the confluence with the Hanbury River contains most of the whitewater and most of the portages. The falls above the confluence with the Elk River must be portaged (1.2 km). Although some canoeists have lined portions of the Thelon Canyon at low water levels, most people should expect to portage 5-6 km around the Canyon. We portaged the falls and the Canyon on the right bank. Depending on paddling skills and water levels, most canoeists should also expect to portage or line several more rapids. In addition to the falls and the Canyon, we portaged 3 short (less than 0.5 km) rapids, lifted over 1 ledge (50 m), and lined one rapid upstream of the Canyon.

The middle section of the River, from the confluence with the Hanbury River to Beverly Lake, generally offers straightforward, pleasant paddling conditions; the current moves, with very little whitewater. The only rapid of any consequence that we encountered, at the Thelon Bluffs, is normally runnable on the inside bend on river right. This section flows through the Thelon Game Sanctuary, and offers the best opportunities for seeing muskoxen.

The last third of the trip, from Beverly Lake to Baker Lake, is all on lakes, except for the 80 km below Aleksektok Rapids. We portaged (2 km) Aleksektok Rapids, although this section has been paddled, particularly at lower water levels. Beverly, Aberdeen, and Schultz Lakes are surrounded by true tundra. Virtually no wood is available for fires. Strong winds will likely prevent travel for days at a time. During some years, ice persists on the lakes until well into summer. Despite these adversities, we very much enjoyed this section of the journey, for it was here that we most commonly saw Inuit tent rings and Inukshuks.

The paddling guide to the Northwest Territories produced by the Canadian Recreational Canoeing Association provides a more detailed river profile for the Thelon River. All paddlers should be aware, however, that rivers change annually and seasonally. We strongly believe that wilderness canoeists must make their own decisions regarding the relative risks of running rapids. We recommend that all paddlers travel the Thelon River as though they are making a first descent.

RECOMMENDED MAPS
(Canadian National Topographic Series)

1:1,000,000

Lockhart River: NP-12/13
Thelon River: NQ-12,13,14

1:250,000

Lynx Lake: 75 J
Beaverhill Lake: 75 I
Hanbury River: 75 P
Clarke River: 65 M
Tammarvi River: 66 D
Beverly Lake: 66 C
Aberdeen Lake: 66 B
Schultz Lake: 66 A
Baker Lake: 56 D

THELON RIVER ITINERARY

Date	Activity/Camping Site	Daily km	Total km
June 28	Fly to Lynx Lake	0	0
June 29	Esker in Lake After 2 Rapids Flowing North	23	23
June 30	Bay After Portage in "U Bend"	19	42
July 1	Sandbar Bay 10 km Before "Falls" Portage	19	61
July 2	North Shore Half Way Between Jim Lake & Elk River	18	79
July 3	Beginning of East-to-West Bend of Flowing Thelon River	64	143
July 4	Anniversary Rest Day	0	143
July 5	Mary Francis River	48	191
July 6	End of Islands Past Sandbar Before Eyeberry Lake	16	207
July 7	North End of Eyeberry Lake	13	220
July 8	Bay North of "Island Rapids" North of Eyeberry Lake	20	240
July 9	Upstream of Two Rapids 5 km South of Thelon Canyon	31	271
July 10	One-half km South of Clarke River	9	280
July 11	Seven km North of Hanbury River	12	292
July 12	Three km North of Cosmos Lake	33	325
July 13	Shore Opposite Hornby Point	34	359
July 14	Bend North Before Thelon River Separates into Channels	60	419
July 15	Lookout Point	43	462
July 16	Bend North to Ursus Islands	34	496
July 17	Five km South of Kigarvi River	36	532
July 18	Entrance to Thelon Bluffs	19	551
July 19	Rest Day at Thelon Bluffs	0	551

July 20	Hoare Point	31	582
July 21	"Double-knoll Point" North of Beverly Lake Cabin	22	604
July 22	Northern Point of Peninsula After "Tyrrell Passage"	31	635
July 23	Layover Day Imposed by NNE Wind	0	635
July 24	Three km Before First Aberdeen Lake Cabin	16	651
July 25	Spit Two km East of Naujatuug River	32	683
July 26	Second Knoll Two km East of "Horn" Turning NNE	26	709
July 27	West Side of Qamanaugaq Bay	38	747
July 28	East Side of Spit on Qamanaugaq Bay	8	755
July 29	Layover Day Imposed by East Wind	0	755
July 30	"Double-arm Bay" on Northeast Side of Whalebone Hill	37	792
July 31	River One-half Way Down. W. Side of Schultz L.Peninsula	32	824
Aug. 1	Schultz Lake Outlet Rapid	33	857
Aug. 2	Below Portage of Aleksektok Rapids	12	869
Aug. 3	Baker Lake	78	947
Aug. 4	Visiting Baker Lake	0	947
Aug. 5	Visiting Baker Lake	0	947
Aug. 6	Fly to Thekulthili Lake	0	947
Aug. 7	Fly to Fort Smith	0	947

FOOD PLANNING

Food planning is not an exact science. What food is taken on a trip depends on the size of the group, and the caloric needs of the individuals as well as their personal food preferences. The length, difficulty and weather conditions expected during the trip must also be assessed. What follows is a sample of the food Michael and I took for dinners on the Thelon River.

After deciding on the recipes and the number of times to repeat each recipe, I created a master table (*see Sample Master Table for Dinners*). For me, a master table of all ingredients for our intended dinners brought order to a daunting task. The master table ensured that no food ingredients were overlooked or forgotten, and also made it easy to pick up ingredients when I found them on sale.

To determine the amount of 'dried' food that could be produced from fresh food, I used comparisons that I had tested personally, or had obtained from books. (*see Sample Fresh-to-Dried Comparison*)

I then compiled a shopping list (*see Sample Shopping List*), and carried it with me, decrementing amounts as I purchased them.

Sample Master Table for Dinners

Each recipe is listed in the first column. Each ingredient is listed in the first row. The first row under each ingredient lists the amount required for one recipe. Next to each recipe is the number of times I intended to repeat that recipe during the trip. The columns below each ingredient contain the total amount of that ingredient needed for the entire time we would spend on the Thelon River (i.e., amount of ingredient x number of times recipe is served). Amounts of ingredients are indicated in Imperial measurements because most of my cookbooks and kitchen measuring equipment are in these units.

SAMPLE MASTER TABLE FOR DINNERS

Recipe/ Ingredients	Pasta	Beef	Beans	Tomatoes (crushed)	Tomato paste	Vegetables	Other
Amount per single recipe	0.5 lbs	1.5 cups (dried ground)	1 cup (cooked dried)			3/4 cups (dried)	
Chile & Cornbread repeat 6 times		9 cups (ground)	6 cups (garbanzo, black beans)	6 cans	6 cans		6 recipes cornbread bannock
Shepherds Pie repeat 4 times		6 cups (ground)			4 cans	3 cups (corn)	3 cups potato flakes
Spagetti repeat 6 times	3 lbs	9 cups (ground)		6 cans			Parmesan cheese 6 pkg spaghetti sauce mix
Stew & Dumplings repeat 4 times		2 lbs (made into jerky)				3 cups (carrots, parsnips)	4 c dried potatoes 4 pkg gravy mix 4 recipes bannock
Totals 20 meals	3 lbs	24 cups ground 2 lbs for jerky	6 cups	12 cans	1 cup (cooked dried)	3 cups (corn) 3 cups (carrots, parsnips)	3 c. potato flakes 4 c. dried potato slices 4 pkg gravy mix 6 pkg spaghetti mix

SAMPLE FRESH-TO-DRIED COMPARISON

FRESH	DRIED
1 pound beef	4 ounces jerky
1 pound ground beef	1.5 cups
16 ounce can black beans	2/3 cup
6 carrots	1 cup
1 pound parsnips	2/3 cup
2 cups kernel corn	1/3 cup

SAMPLE SHOPPING LIST

Spaghetti	3 lbs
Ground beef	16 lbs
Beef for jerky	2 lbs
Beans (garbonzo)	5 (16 oz) cans
Beans (black)	5 (16 oz) cans
Tomatoes (crushed)	12 cans
Tomatoes (paste)	10 cans
Corn	18 cups
Carrots	12
Parsnips	1.25 lbs
Potato flakes	24 oz
Potato slices (dried scalloped mix)	32 oz
Gravy mix	4 pkg
Spaghetti sauce mix	6 pkg

ABOUT THE AUTHORS

Kathleen and Michael first hiked together in the mountains of southern British Columbia in 1977. Since taking up canoeing in 1987, they have devoted most of their free time to gaining paddling experience in southern British Columbia on a wide variety of rivers, including the Capilano, Cheakamus, Chilliwack, Coldwater, Cowichan, Nicola, Seymour, Squamish, Similkameen and Tulameen.

Their first wilderness adventure in the Northwest Territories occurred in 1990, when they paddled three weeks and 565 km down the Nahanni River from the Moose Ponds to Blackstone Landing on the Liard River. After their Thelon River trip in 1993, Kathleen and Michael returned to the north in 1995 to spend 4 weeks travelling 650 km down the Coppermine River from the site of historic Fort Enterprise to the Inuit community of Kugluktuk (formerly Coppermine) on the Arctic Coast. Two summers later, Michael and Kathleen descended the Seal River in Northern Manitoba, where they spent 3 weeks paddling 300 km from Shethanei Lake to the western shore of Hudson Bay. For their most recent wilderness adventure, Michael and Kathleen spent the winter of 1999 (January-June) living in a 1-room cabin north of the Arctic Circle in the Northwest Territories.

In her non-paddling life, Kathleen is responsible for Document Strategies in ITServices at the University of British Columbia. Michael is also employed at UBC, as Associate Professor of Grassland Ecology in the Faculty of Agricultural Sciences. Kathleen and Michael are both certified by the Recreational Canoeing Association of British Columbia as flat-water canoeing instructors, and regularly present slide-shows on wilderness canoeing to many groups throughout the Vancouver Area.